Saved by Grace

Saved by Grace

Marc E. Willis

authorHOUSE®

AuthorHouse™ LLC
1663 Liberty Drive
Bloomington, IN 47403
www.authorhouse.com
Phone: 1-800-839-8640

Published by AuthorHouse   10/28/2013

ISBN: 978-1-4817-6463-6 (sc)
ISBN: 978-1-4817-6462-9 (e)

Library of Congress Control Number: 2013911009

Contents

PREFACE

In this book, you will find many oracles in understanding faith, the substance to believe and deal with individuals that are facing physical and mental challenges. This book will also help bring a great level of understanding to those of us who find their disabling abilities a great challenge.

The Bible says that faith without works is dead, so I encourage all those that choose to fight their afflictions to engage yourself in a spiritual light and those that take the opportunity to do so will find themselves strengthened, not only in their bodies, but most importantly, their mind and soul.

The Bible says that the name of the Lord is a strong tower (Prov. 18:10), and as we understand it, a tower represents a safe haven. As a hawk makes its nest up in the highest tree, it only does so because of its safety. As the smallest bird makes its nest in the highest tree, it does so because being low to the ground would make it an easy prey to all predators that roam the land seeking to devour.

God is our tower which represents that highest point, and by God being that strong tower, He's able to keep a careful watch over us from all harm and danger that the enemy may bring our way.

Faith is the substance of things hoped for and the evidence of things not seen (Heb. 11:1). The Bible says that there is a cure for everything under the sun.

REMEMBER
The spirit of a man will sustain him in sickness,
But who can bear a broken spirit?
Prov. 18:14

A TESTIMONY FOR BABY GRACIE

My name is Tiara Debardlabon and I am the mother of two beautiful daughters. This testimony starts in 2012, before baby Gracie was born. This was supposed to have been one of the most happiest times of my life, but on this particular day, 18 weeks into my pregnancy, I went for an ultrasound to find out the sex of my baby.

While I anticipated a boy, but would have been just as happy for a girl, my whole world came to a shocking standstill. When the doctor informed me that my baby, which would be a girl, had a abdominal wall defect, which meant that the baby's liver was developing on the outside of her body.

The doctors informed me that it would probably be best if I aborted the baby. Now, abortion is something that I'm not a fan of, but I listened to every doctor and physician that had a medical opinion for me. Everything came back to terminating this pregnancy. I was very hurt and filled with despair. I couldn't find any doctor that would shed some glimmer of hope for my child, but I pressed forward anyhow. I made the decision to bring forth life. I began to look at all at what God said and what God is, and I knew that my child would make it to this side of the world.

Life became more difficult now, because during this pregnancy, not only did I have to worry about what would be, not only did I have to pray for God's favor and change, but I still had to go to work every day, and that was not easy, but with Christ, I pushed forward.

I must say that through the days and the weeks and the months of my pregnancy, my life was truly filled with strenuous doctor visits every single month, as well as dealing with a strenuous work environment where I was constantly on my feet moving from one end of a medical clinic to the other, placing all of my worry for my child's safety, healing and protection in God's hands, to focus on the patients that were right here in my care. Needless to say, it was very difficult, but I was determined to see it all through.

As the work days got longer and harder, my due date got closer and closer. I was so afraid and anxious at the same time. Still hearing the worse from the doctors, and even some friends, it was God and my family and a few others, that encouraged me and let me know that everything would be alright. Now, let me remind you that I was told that I would have to have a cesarean, because the baby's liver was still outside of her body. The doctors were afraid that if I tried to give birth naturally, the liver would rupture.

As the doctors prepared me for the c-section, I started having contractions and they were coming very fast. Before I could be given an epidural or anything for pain, I felt the urge to push and all of a sudden, out came Gracie. The doctors were surprised that even though I didn't have the c-section, Gracie came out with everything intact. Her liver was still on the outside of her body. Although now I had passed one grueling ordeal, I knew in my heart that there would be many more to come. The Bible says that the race is not given to the swift, but to those who endure to the end. I made up in my mind that I would fight the good fight of faith.

The day after Gracie was born, it was discovered that she had a diaphramic hernia which caused her not to be able to breath. She was immediately transported to Eglestone Children's Hospital to undergo surgery to correct the problem. I was told that Gracie might not even make it to the hospital, but I knew Doctor Jesus.

Four days later, the surgeons came in and said that they had to put a tube in Gracie's throat because she was not able to breath. It seemed that my walls of prayers would never cease. Praying to God became a tireless task, but it was something that I had to do. You see, I knew from the very beginning that this child would be a special child, and everything that she goes through is only setting her up to be that much more remarkable in life.

Gracie's surgery had been successful. The doctors had put her liver back in and stitched her diaphragm. They also removed the tube from her throat to see if she was able to breath on her own. Gracie did very well on her own for about a week, then the doctors had to put the tube back in her throat. My excitement to her getting well was short-lived when they informed me that she would need a tracheotomy.

A few weeks later, the tracheotomy was performed and I must say, still against all odds, my love, my heart, my baby, Gracie is taking to it well. She smiles when she hears my voice. She's very alert and living. My baby is on a constant morphine drip and she will be off soon because she will be coming home.

I have already seen the hands of God move on my child. God has already shown me that He is large and in charge. As my baby Grace and myself move forward through these most rocky times, I do know and believe that God will always be there for us to see her grow up into a beautiful and healthy woman, only to look back as an adult, with no recollection of these moments, but only to say, thank you mom and thank you God, for your saving grace.

This is our testimony.

MARC WILLIS'S STORY

My name is Marc Willis. I am from Pomona, California as well as the author of this awesome book. My testimony begins in 1992, when I was first diagnosed with diabetes. This is the first time I asked the question, am I saved by grace? The reason I asked this question is because now I somewhat understood the sickness my mother had.

Diabetes has always been told to me that it, along with high blood pressure was a silent killer. These two diseases are hereditary and although I know and believe that they can be fought and controlled with medication, I also believe that through prayer and God's great belief factor, these diseases can be overcome. Many times I felt that God's hand was strong inside of me. I just believed that while my mother lay on her deathbed, my prayers could have delivered her, but because I neglected to lay hands on her and pray, it showed me that my belief wasn't at the point where she could have been healed.

You see, to be healed takes a certain amount of belief in what you are trying to change. You must act on what you believe and you must believe on what you're acting on. God speaks life and God said that life and death are in the power of the tongue. So, we must first believe that life is in the tongue. We must not waiver in our faith when we begin to speak it. I see things right now in my own health that will possibly someday bring me to end of my walk. If I take all of my understanding and begin to believe in something different, such as living 77 years as God has promised, that is very possible.

Now don't get me wrong. There are other factors involved when it comes to speaking life inside of you. Understanding it's just one of those things that you must believe in when you're praying because that way your praying won't be wrong. You must conduct yourself in a way that is operable to what your faith needs to move in.

My diabetes really started taking a toll on my body very quickly and I was steadily growing weaker. It seemed that everything I did was increasingly difficult to accomplish. When I ran, I would get tired quickly. It seemed as though my energy level had dropped completely. I began to lose weight without even making an effort and I was losing my appetite. I had increased pain in my legs and the more I worked out, more pain would come with it. At this time, I didn't see any problems with my eyes, my heart, my kidneys or even my blood circulation, but as I now look back, those problems were growing at a very slow and silent rate.

After my mother died, I got married and that marriage produced three lovely children Stepvon, who is the oldest, Montreyll who is the middle child, and Nicholas who is the youngest. The birth of my children in itself, was the greatest blessing I could ever receive. It was also one of the most saddest moments because my children were born right after my parents passed. I didn't know I would find part of God's grace in the birth of my children, but I did and now I can say from my parents death came life. It was also at this time that my sister, who has been trying to have children for years, finally was able to give birth to two beautiful girls, Jordyn and Cortlyn.

The spirit of our parents rested in the bosoms of our children. My three boys were truly a blessing to me. With the death of my parents and looking towards my future, my kids gave me a whole new outlook on life. Not only did I have to live for me, but I needed to live for my children. My children are a very big part of that grace that holds my life. In other words, my children are and will always be part of that cure that I so desperately desire in my life.

Back in 1997 when I was traveling between Los Angeles and Chicago, I was bit by a poisonous spider called a Brown Recluse. The Brown Recluse is one of the most deadliest spiders known to man. I had seen and felt some type of sore on the back of my leg, but I didn't pay much attention. As I traveled from state to state and from place to place, the pain on the back of leg became more irritating and more intense. Because I didn't know the exact date or place where I was bitten, it had to have been about a week from the time I started to feel the pain in my leg that I knew that I had been bitten by something. I had this huge red sore growing on the back of my leg and along with that came the most unbearable pain. If you blew on it, it brought me to tears and if you touched it, I would want to fight you. The pain was just that bad.

When I couldn't take the pain any longer, I went to the hospital while I was in Chicago. That was when I was told about the culprit that was causing my pain—the Brown Recluse Spider. The bite from this type of spider can kill you in one of three ways—the poison can either eat the flesh off your body or it can attack the bone marrow or it can cause paralysis throughout the whole body. The one that bit me carried the flesh eating virus, so once the poison had gotten into my bloodstream, things happened in stages.

Within two days, I couldn't walk and within three days, paralysis set in and within four days, I was losing the flesh around the area where I was bitten. Within 7 days, I was looking at amputation or worse, death. The poison was steadily eating at my flesh and my sugar glucose level was in the 400-500 range and that was not good because nothing could heal with a level that high. I had decided that if I came into the hospital with two legs, I was leaving the hospital with two legs.

The doctors tried many different things to try to combat the poison and it was difficult to do for many reasons. For one, I was a diabetic and my glucose level was out of control, which made it hard for me to heal. Another thing was that before it was discovered what type of spider bit me, the doctors had a hard time trying to find an anti-viral anecdote. So, I got worse and so did the pain.

Because I refused to have my leg amputated, the doctors brought in a specialist who had a new anti-viral anecdote to try. This anecdote had the same antibodies that are found in a pig's immune system. As it turned out, this seemed to do the trick. God is truly in control!

Within two days, the effects from the poison began to subside. The only physical scar that the doctors told me would be visible was the ulcer on the leg itself. My leg was five times smaller than the other one was and it could not support my weight. My rehabilitation lasted about five months, which was enough time for me to regain enough size on my leg to sustain my weight, as well as my mobility and athletic ability.

God said that there is a cure for everything under the sun. Even through my selfishness, my greed and anything that is the opposite of what God is. He still did what God does best and that is bless. In the midst of all that I had gone through and the things that I would go through, my faith kept my head above water, and I knew then, just as I know now, that all things work together for those that love the Lord.

Now I truly had to love the Lord because not only did I have to nurse myself back together, but because of the effects of the poison, I lost an extreme amount of weight, and you know family. They can be the worse. Instead of consoling me, I was asked if I had AIDS. Why do people always assume the worse when someone loses weight? Don't let your ignorance be your judge.

Looking at my faith and building it up with scriptures like, "For God is the same today, yesterday and forever." The same way He saved Jonah trapped in the belly of the whale, He saved me. Just as He healed the woman with an issue of blood, He healed me and He has continued to heal me. Therefore, greater is He that is in me, than He that is in the world.

Later, while working on a construction job through my construction business, my eyes began to fail. A friend of mine took me to the eye doctor. When that doctor examined me and informed me that I was losing my sight, the only thing I could say was, "Lord, am I not saved by Your Grace?" Everything and anything that could happen to me at that point probably could have been the best thing for me. I was placing myself in a very bad position. The person that took me to see the doctor was the same person I stole $7,000.00 from—not physically. My company was contracted by this individual to do some work for her. The total bill was $1,500.00, and I didn't completely keep my end of the bargain. I was wrong and wrong is wrong, no matter how you slice it. I know that I owe this person and it seemed that I am paying with my life's abilities—among other things.

I ask God for his forgiveness for every deal that I made in the wrong spirit or the wrong agenda. I sometimes think that I am going through what I'm going through because of some of the things that I've done in my life and to others. It could be my season to go through something or maybe it's God's way of showing me where I need to be. Whatever the reason, I can say one thing—God has my attention. I have truly atoned to my sins and I'm truly acknowledging all those that I did wrong and I now realize that God is much bigger than I am and whatever God wants, God will have. So, all of the things that I do, I do it in the name of Jesus Christ.

Now, during the time that I was going through my eye situation, I was alone. I had gotten a divorce from my second wife, but I still had a few male and female friends that I called on from to time to help me. I had some corrective surgery done but that only aided in my eyesight getting worse. Three months from that very first visit to the eye doctor, both eyes were failing me miserably and two months later, I was totally blind in both eyes.

From that moment on, life for me became very difficult. I had to rely on others now to take me to the doctor and to run simple errands. I even thought that I would forget what my children looked like. It was very difficult for me to pick them up or go visit them and slowly but surely, most of the people that I thought were my friends, they stopped coming around.

Despite what I was going through with my blindness, I never cried nor asked God why. During that first year of my sickness, I remember going to at least 15 different ophthalmologists and none of them could tell me why my sight had failed me. I did find out later that my vision problems were caused by high blood pressure.

It seemed as though people didn't understand my blindness. It was very difficult to get to the store, my doctor's appointments or any other place I needed to go. I would often tell people if they wanted to know what it is like to be blind, I would ask them to close their eyes, place their hands over their eyes and walk backward for as long as they can. I guarantee you that after you get through bumping into things and falling on your butt, you will have a very good idea of what it's like to be blind.

Literally overnight, I went from being able to see and having a full life to becoming blind and having to depend on others for help. It had been several months since I had become blind and I was getting used to it. Just as I was getting used to being blind, if you can get used to such a thing, I started having stomach pains that were becoming more and more severe. After many trips to the emergency room and many tests performed to find out what was going on, I was finally diagnosed with End Stage Renal Failure. I had to go on dialysis and I had to go on dialysis now!

I was undone after receiving that news. It's bad enough that I can't see, I have go on dialysis too? What was going on? What was God trying to do in my life? Once again, if God was trying to get my attention, He had it now.

Now, I just didn't agree to going on dialysis right away, even though my doctors kept telling me I would die if I didn't go on dialysis soon. I just was not going to agree to it. I hadn't heard from God about that. As far as I was concerned, I was not making any moves until I heard from God. Do you know that the doctor even sent me to a psychiatrist because they thought something was wrong with my mind? My family members thought I was nuts for not wanting to go on dialysis right away. I know they didn't want me to be hurt anymore than I already was, but I was waiting to here from God.

Well, after much crying and praying and talking to God, I finally conceded and got on dialysis and I have been on dialysis for the last six years. It has not been as bad as I thought it would be and God is constantly showing me things about myself that I never knew. I am constantly learning and growing. Even as I continue with my dialysis treatments three times a week, God has shown me that an end will come to all of this. I will be victorious in all of this because I know that God has never left nor forsaken me.

Now even though I was on dialysis, God saw fit to deliver me from one of my demons, which I will be forever grateful for His mercy. I mentioned earlier that I had been a Type 2 diabetic since 1992. In 2006, God healed me from diabetes and I have never needed insulin from that time forward. I give all praises to God! I believe if you are stepping out on faith for a thing, God will meet you right where you are at and take you to that next level.

Now, at this time, I began to think that everything would be fine. Right when I got healed from diabetes, I would soon be hit with something so devastating that I thought I would never recover from this one.

I had to go to the hospital because I had an ear infection. My ear was hurting me so bad and I didn't know what to do. I was in the hospital emergency room for over four hours while the nurses and doctors were taking different tests to find out what was causing my ear to ache. Well, to make a long story short, my ear ache turned into a 8 valve bypass! Don't ask me how—that just the way it was explained to me. It was supposed to be preventive surgery. You see, I never had a problem with cholesterol, and I jogged and exercised every day and I roller skated almost every day and I never had any pain whatsoever, in my chest. I never had a heart attack nor any heart problems in my life!

You would think that through each of these illnesses, a normal person would have gone crazy or would have just given up on themselves and God. I always think of a phrase that I have heard through the years over and over and that is, God will not put more on you than you can handle.

Obviously, my Lord and Savior Jesus Christ must have known that I could handle my sicknesses without a problem. I know that it was only because of God's grace and His protection, that I have made it through each and every situation unharmed. I am covered by the blood of Jesus. I might have a few scars, but I am still standing. I felt that this would soon become my life altering, faith building testimony. You see during the time battling dialysis, blindness and severe pain in my chest, I was unaware of a stroke that had taken place, which caused my right eyelid to shut. Now I never knew it was shut because of being blind, until someone brought it to my attention.

Life was very hard. Having paralysis throughout the lower portion of my body, not being able to put on my shoes, socks or even my pants. Always needing some form of assistance. Many times I felt like just giving up. I knew that I had been through enough things already, but I still had this fear that God would allow more to come.

In many ways, I still have that fear. I struggle very hard not to be crippled. I like to show as much as I can that I will and must rise above all that has hindered my walk and all that has hindered my capability to succeed in life.

It seems that the saga never lets up. Every three months, I have to have surgery in the upper part of my body to drain fluid that cannot be removed through dialysis. Even that surgery can't be done too many times because even that in itself, brings its own set of problems. Still, I'm going to continue to pray and move forward in the abilities that God has so gracefully blessed me with, whether it be my comedy, my music, my writing or any other endeavor I choose to explore.

I exalt You, my God the King,
and praise Your name forever and ever.

Psalm 145:1

MY FAMILY TESTIMONY

In the summer of 1979, my Aunt Betty and Uncle Nate Bowers embarked upon a journey that would take them from the coast of Los Angeles, CA to the shores of Atlanta, Ga. Aunt Betty is the oldest out of three sisters: Gwen, Helen and herself. Atlanta, Georgia is where they felt their two children, Gail and Christopher would receive a better quality of life.

Back in the late 70's and early 80's, Atlanta was an up and coming metropolis. A city that was known for its peach trees and southern hospitality, Atlanta was a city that was thriving on the brink of great success. There were more trees than there were houses and buildings. There were hardly any four-lane roads. No street carried a sidewalk and the mayor of Atlanta at that time was Maynard Jackson. At any time, anywhere in the city, you might find Nate and Betty Bowers driving their Restaurant on Wheels.

You see, back then, there were very few, if any, food service trucks operating. Now I don't mean the small food truck, I mean the great big food truck. They were really moving and shaking back then. Their two children, Gail and Chris were going to the very best schools that Atlanta had to offer.

Nate and Betty Bowers were doing very well as entrepreneurs in the great city we simply title, "The A." At that time, there was also a grim and dark cloud hovering Atlanta. You see, our young kids were mysteriously being taken off the street—kidnapped and being killed. A young man by the name of Wayne Williams was convicted of killing 27 black children, mostly boys between October 1979 and May 1981. Williams was sentenced to life in prison. People were really afraid back then and all young people had a curfew until the perpetrator was caught.

Our family in other states were aware of what was happening in Atlanta, Georgia and we were so afraid that something would happen to our auntie's children, Gail and Chris. God seemed to keep them in safe hands. After all, Aunt Betty became the glue of the family. Sometime in the late 80's, Auntie Betty had been dealt her first blow. Her youngest sister Gwen had passed. This was very disturbing, but Betty had been a fighter all of her life. You see, Betty's mother had died when she was just 15 years old and she had to help her father raise both her sisters. She became a mother like figure at an early age. Now in 1995, Betty would lose her second sister, Helen, and it shook Betty's world once again. Many years had gone by and the Bower children were now in college.

TESTIMONY #1

Marc E. Willis

Life was a sweet joy for them at that time. Chris would go on to graduate from college and get married to a beautiful woman. Gail would go on to graduate from college and marry her handsome prince and bring forth three beautiful boys, Langston, Matthew and Caleb. Now one of the things I am most grateful for is that my Uncle Nate and Aunt Betty became the center of our family. For all holidays and special events, she would always prepare the best dinners and all the family would assemble at her home. Family seemed to be very important to her. She would put these dinners together all by herself, not once asking the family to help or to bring anything. It was always just come and bring your appetite. If any of her sisters' children had any problems with anything, she would always be the first we would call and she was always the one that would offer help.

That would be just like her to pick up where our mothers left off. Now at this time, my Uncle Nate and his wife Betty were growing older and at the same time gaining more wisdom than ever before. It was then in the year of our Lord, 2001, when my Aunt Betty received a call while in Florida, that her son had just died on his motorcycle. This ravished all her thoughts and intellect. Not knowing exactly what happened, set off a cataclysmic chain of anguish and anxiety inside of her.

They hurried back as quick as possible to Georgia to face the reality of what's been already told to them. Their only son, at the age of 25 had been killed while riding his motorcycle on I-20 late one night.

The rest of the family had been notified and all the family could think about was our Uncle Nate and Auntie Betty. You see, Chris was the baby boy of all the children. He was only second to me, Marc Willis. I knew then that we had just lost a very big part of the foundation that the parents of Chris Bowers had established.

It was very difficult for my Aunt Betty. This would be a challenge that she would not soon overcome. As a nephew, what do you say? What do you do? I always thought how could I give of myself to help ease the pain that she and my uncle Nate would feel, from this day forward.

Well, all I know is to continue to love both of them even more now and offer myself to them more than ever before. In 2007, the evils of this world showed its side again. My aunt, Betty Bowers, was diagnosed with breast cancer and also had to have both of her knees replaced, all in the same year. After her knee surgery, Betty spent two months in rehab. Once again, this sent shock waves in the family and more so, it troubled this primarily healthy woman.

To have lost your only son and then to hear that you have this deadly disease, sure doesn't make life easier. Through all the treatments and preventative therapy, a decision was made for a mastectomy. Through study and the history of this disease, it was decided that she have a double mastectomy. The surgery was planned and executed and all of the cancer was removed. It has been six years since her mastectomy and her knee replacement. My family and I am proud to say that at 76 years of age, my auntie is moving better, doing things better and driving better than ever before. The same can be said about my Uncle, Mr. Nate Bowers.

On behalf of our family, this is our testimony.

Hallelujah!
My soul, praise the Lord.
I will praise the Lord all my life;
I will sing to the Lord as long as I live.

Psalm 146:1-2

SAVED TWICE

by
Rosa Lewis

One of the greatest blessings to man is accepting Jesus as his personal Savior. Another one is marrying the love of your life. As far back as I can remember I have had God in my life. As a little girl, I remember taking my youngest sister to church. My mother would allow us to walk to the church that was a couple of blocks away. With everything I knew, as a little child, I loved God. As I grew older, my knowledge and love for God grew.

When I became a young adult, I did not leave the church or let go of my Christian values. I married my high school sweetheart and I felt like I was one of the happiest people in the world . . . at least in Georgia. Life has a way of throwing you curve balls you are not equipped to handle. As my husband and I grew older and worked in the church and for the Lord, we faced many challenges and obstacles. One may be quick to say that when you work for the Lord, the devil will sure get busy. Yes, that is true, but sometimes, we are our own worst demonic influence.

My husband was good at most things that he did. He quickly went up the ladder in the ranks of the church denomination of which we were members. Something happened with him that changed him into a person I was no longer acquainted with. Being a woman of faith, I prayed, fasted and believed God for a miracle to change and convert my husband, the Church Conference Official. I suffered so many things at his hand that I sometimes wondered what had I done for me to be punished and treated so badly. I felt like God did not hear my prayers. I even felt like giving up.

One day the Spirit of God spoke to me and said this journey is not built on feeling, but on the fact that you have faith in a living God. At that moment, I told God, I was not going to let go of Him (God) until he blesses me. After much prayer, I was convinced that it was time for the divorce that I had tried to avoid for countless years. One of the last things I told my husband was "you reap what you sow; I hope you are able to handle what you have sown." I am not an advocate of divorce. I believe God desires for His children to live in harmony, to forgive, and for families to survive and thrive. God has laid out in his word the reasons he permits divorce. But even with that, he desires that forgiveness and wholeness is restored. So it's so very important to be prayerful and lead by the Spirit of God, not only when contemplating divorce, but in every aspect of your life. In everything we should acknowledge God and He will direct our paths.

TESTIMONY #2

After my divorce, I was a brand new woman. Once again I felt the innocence and the peace of God I had known as a youngster. It was so awesome that at first I didn't know what it was . . . until God told me it was PEACE. Oh how I praised God even more. I had gone back to college as a nontraditional student and life was really great until that night. I worked a full time job during the day and went to school at night. As I was getting out of the car that night, I looked up to see a masked man leaning over the top of a car with a gun aimed at me. My first thought was that someone was out robbing in the middle of the night. I am a small person in stature and quite timid, but one thing God did not give me was a spirit of fear. As I raised my hands to say I didn't have any money, the masked man started shooting, without a word or movement.

Several shots rang out. I don't know how many. But when the fourth one hit me, I went down. I fell to the ground and when I came to; I felt the blood flowing out. I began to talk to God. I asked him why now? I'm finally happy. I had lived in hell so long with a man I thought loved me. I had struggles on the job, with people, with finances; just with life's struggles. But now, I don't have those stressors. I had been recently divorced. I'm almost finished with college. I will close on my own house in a few weeks. Lord why now, I'm finally happy. But then I paused for a quick second and said, "Lord thank you for this short period of happiness." I closed my eyes to die, but God my Father, said it's not time. My Father told me to "get up."

I replied that I wasn't going to get up because he might still be there and finish me off. He said get up or you will surely die. At that instance, I made the decision to be obedient and get up. When I did, Jesus stopped death in its tracks; just like He did when he stopped dying on the cross to save the thief who was hanging next to him. I got up and <u>ran</u> the apartment door to my friend where I was living. The police and ambulance arrived quickly because people had reported a shooting in the area. They worked diligently to find the bullet entrances and to keep me from going into shock.

The next thing I remember is waking up in ICU in a local rehab center unable to move anything but my head. I could not talk. I was hooked up to machines, tubes, and pumps. After gaining consciousness, I found out that I had been in a coma for almost two months and had swollen up 3 times my normal size and had endured several surgeries. My family told me later that the hospital had done all they could for me and had sent me to the rehab center to die. My sister told the doctor when he called them in to inform them that I was going to die, she called him a lie and she didn't want to talk to him anymore. She knew I was a fighter and I was not going to die.

This fighter was now out of the coma, but is in ICU and can't do anything but think and pray. I was finally moved to a regular room. The doctors and police talked to me and asked what happened. When I told them, everyone was in amazement because with the injuries I sustained, I should not have been able to get up, let alone get up and run. With much prayer, faith, hard work, and more surgeries and strenuous rehab, God continued to work miracles in my life. In this one incidence, He worked countless miracles in my life and others. His Spirit resides in me in such a divine manner. He stopped death, imparted me with forgiveness, sustained me, healed me, and showed others his miracle working power

Marc E. Willis

in a person they could identify with. So many other blessings resulted from this. He showed me that He loved me more than I even knew. I knew that God loved me. He loves all of his creation. Oh, but how he showed me in a manner that I didn't even know God would show this insignificant human whom Satan had tried to destroy.

He used my ex-husband who had been the love of my life to try to destroy me. When he couldn't do it emotionally or spiritually, he tried to do it physically by trying to take my life. The masked man behind the gun was my ex-husband.

I am so glad that neither death, life, nor principalities, things past, present, nor things to come, nor any person or circumstances are able to separate me from the love of God which is in Christ Jesus. My Father has restored my health. Though I was shot four times, I don't know what it feels like to be shot. God took the sting out of the bullets. I did not ask for pain medicine in the hospital because there was no pain. Praise God! God kept me in my right mind. I kept my mind stayed on Him.

I don't have to have anyone to feed me or wheel me around. Even with the injuries, countless surgeries and rehab sessions, I went back at work full time within 11 months. I graduated from college with a BA Degree and with honors. I have had two promotions on my job. I don't harbor hatred in my heart. There are so many other blessings. Because of his goodness and his grace, I can tell of his Protection, his Presence, and his Power. I have truly been Saved by his Grace, not once, but twice; when he saved me from the power of sin by coming into my life as Lord and Savior, and when he saved be from the power of death.

*The one who follows instruction is
on the path to life,
but the one who rejects correction
goes astray*

Proverbs 10:17

THE TESTIMONY OF ANGELA WALKER

HEAVEN HAS NO SIN AND SIN HAS NO GLORY

My story begins in 1993. I was a member of a large church in Atlanta, Georgia. My pastor was popular and the congregation loved him and the messages that he preached. I had been a member there for several years and I loved the pastor too. Only, my type of love was not what you would call spiritual. You see, the pastor and I were having an affair. Yes, I knew he was married and yes, I knew he had children, but at the time, neither one of us was caring about those things. I gained a lot of things as a result of being in a relationship with this married man. We tried to keep everything under wraps and he showered me with so many gifts and so many favors.

I tell you, I had a new car, a condo that he paid for, the best clothes that money could buy and of course, anytime I needed money, I didn't have to worry because I was always taken care of. This went on like that for a few years.

Well as we all know, all sinful things must come to an end. I don't know if the devil was cashing in on the deal we made or if God knew that it was time to rectify the problem. It wouldn't be long before things took a more drastic turn. I do know that I got pregnant by this married man. I didn't know what to do at first. I prayed and I cried and I cried and I prayed. Finally, I decided that I could not deal with the charade anymore. I told the pastor I was pregnant, in which he replied that is wasn't his.

I have never felt so humiliated in all my life. Because I was having a baby by a married pastor, I eventually lost all of my friends, my family made me an outcast, the church told me I was not welcome there anymore, it was just an awful time. I do know that God was preparing me for something. I knew I had done the right thing by bringing the affair to the forefront—and of course, the pastor denied all of it!

Well, I carried the baby full term, but unfortunately it was a stillborn delivery. I was not even upset. How could I be? I had defiled the bed of a married man and wife and not only that, he was supposed to be a man of God.

In 1995, which was about a year after I had lost the cars, the homes, the money, the vacations, the man, the baby, and of course, family and friends, I found HIV. I was devastated and after some extensive research, I discovered that I got HIV from my old lover, my pastor. Wow! Yet another thing to deal with. I also started noticing that slowly but surely, every single thing that I had obtained from that relationship, was gone.

TESTIMONY #3

All the things that I stole trying to have possession of someone who didn't belong to me started going away.

To make a long story short, the pastor died from AIDS about two years later in 1997. As he got sicker and sicker, he would call me every day to apologize to me for what he had done. He told me that he was afraid of what his congregation would say and he knew he should have said something earlier.

I continued to ask God for forgiveness every day. I didn't want to die and I knew I had learned my lesson. I kept going to the doctor for the next two years with the same result until one day, I went to the doctor to receive my lab results for HIV and to my surprise and to God's glory, I found out that the test this time was negative for HIV! It was completely gone and no one could explain it.

Praises be to the Father!

Of course, I was left with a calling card. Since my immune system was weak during the time I was positive for HIV, my kidneys went bad and I had to go on dialysis. To me, that is a small price to pay for destroying my spiritual life. God had mercy on me and just like Paul had to deal with his "thorn in his side," so must I. I consider myself saved by His grace. God could have taken my life just as he has allowed with the pastor, but he didn't. Every time I see the marks on my arm from the dialysis graft and every time I go to dialysis for my treatments, I am reminded of God's grace and mercy. I am stronger for my experience. I am wiser because of it.

This is my life altering, faith building testimony.

Therefore the Lord is waiting
to show you mercy
and is rising up to show you compassion,
for the Lord is a just God.
All who wait patiently for Him are happy.

Isaiah 30:18

MY STORY

By
Anna Dixon

It begins with me having a headache for three or more days, when a voice came to me saying "Pack your bag. You are going to the hospital and you are going to stay for a while." I called my youngest daughter and told her to come get me. She came, but as most young folks, she wanted to know why.

After running tests and my blood pressure being 227/119 and my blood sugar being high, I was admitted to the hospital. I don't remember anything else, but when I woke up, I had a big bandage on my chest. I was told that my kidneys weren't working and that I had kidney failure. I had a catheter connected to my veins, close to my heart, so I had to be careful.

On May 3, 2006, I had my first dialysis treatment. It was set up for me to have treatments on Mondays, Wednesdays and Fridays. About two to three weeks after that, I couldn't keep anything on my stomach and coming in weighing about 250 pounds, I was losing a lot weight. My nurse would refer to me as, "walking death on a stick."

After about two or three weeks, I had to go to the hospital again because I had an infection. I got that cleared up and I changed to a dialysis center that was close to home. Everything seemed alright for a while, but then I started having trouble with low blood pressure. One day after having a treatment, I was walking to the scales to be weighed and I blacked out. I fell down and broke my foot.

I now started doing home dialysis and things went well for a while. I was now doing the stationary bike, which I like to do very much. I got sick again and had to go back to the hospital and this time I stayed in ICU for three days, had different kinds of infections and a blood clot in my left leg. The doctors had to remove the dialysis port from my stomach and I had to return to hemodialysis. A new graft had to be put in my leg because there was no other place to put it since my right side had clotted up.

I was supposed to have a procedure done. I take Coumadin, so I was supposed to stop taking it and take Lovenox shots. While I was in the hospital for the procedure, the doctors discovered I was bleeding in my stomach from taking the Lovenox shots. Having trouble with my stomach caused my pancreas to act up and I found out that my gall bladder needed to come out.

After going through all of those things, in July 2010, I was supposed to have a graft put in my right leg. I went to the hospital to have this outpatient procedure done and it turned into a nightmare.

TESTIMONY #4

19

When I awoke from the procedure, the thigh where the graft was supposed to be was as large as both of my thighs put together. I spent some time in the hospital and spent four months in a rehab center because I had to learn to walk all over again.

I prayed each and every time I had to go through something and I know that the Lord was with me and I am very thankful.

The Lord reigns! Let the people tremble.

He is enthroned above the cherubim.

Let the earth quake.

Psalm 99:1

THE TESTIMONY OF JONE WILKERSON

JONAH IN THE BELLY OF THE WHALE

My name is Jone Wilkerson and I am 65 years old. This is my testimony.

Last year, six of us were on a fishing trawler, fishing off the coast of Northern California and we were out there trying to catch some fish. A lot of us were depending on this catch to help us pay up on some bills. Some of the fisherman were really behind, so this particular fishing trip meant a lot.

On that day, the sea began to produce gale-forced winds. The waters were so rugged that the entire crew felt that it would be best to turn about and bring the boat back into shore. This was to be a very important fishing haul. You see, we had a goal of two tons of fish to catch, and that was a goal that we desperately needed to reach. The waves of the ocean began to batter the boat extremely hard, and the crew and I felt that it wouldn't be long until the water began to enter our vessel. We still had a feeling of hope because after all, we were on a strong built boat and we also had state of the art safety equipment for this sort of thing. We had a water pump to safety take the water out of the boat before it became too dangerous. We came upon a large school of fish and threw the nets out to catch them. I never saw so many fish in all my life. All the nets were full and the crew was really happy.

At this time, the boat began to take on water. We were advised to turn up the water pumps full speed. In fact, the boat was taking on so much water, that the boat began to tilt as if it was going to turn over. The water was very rough and we were really having a tough time keeping the water from filling up the boat. It was starting to sink fast from all of the water in it.

Because the boat was tilting so, it was very hard for me to keep my balance and I slipped and fell toward the anchor. I hit the anchor so hard that my leg was impaled by the hook of the anchor. I was in a lot of pain and I was bleeding quite a bit. All of a sudden I thought of another danger. There were sharks in the water and all they had to do was to smell my blood and it might be all over for me.

Well, as I had guessed, the sharks were smelling my blood and it was more than one shark coming our way. By this time we were in the water and we had to get out of it. Someone radioed the Coast Guard and they were on their way with helicopters. In the meantime, we had to figure out what to do about those sharks.

TESTIMONY #5

Well, that large school of fish that we caught was still on the boat, so what we did was let that catch go back into the water, nets and all. The sharks attention was turned away from us and their attention went to the fish, which they ate. I mean they ate every bit of fish that was in that net! I guess they were pretty full, because a few of them came our direction, but they didn't bother us. That was a blessing!

The Coast Guard did finally come and they aided us in getting out of the water. After all, we didn't want to wait for the sharks to get hungry again. I was taken to the hospital so that my leg could be mended and a couple of the other crew members were there to have a doctor look at their scrapes and cuts. It was really an interesting day.

After all had been said and done, we had lost a $95,000.00 boat. We had lost approximately $300,000.00 in fish and equipment and all five guys, including the captain down to the youngest mate, survived with just cuts and bruises. We were relieved to be on board a rescue ship on our way home.

Weeks later, the captain informed us that the insurance company would be purchasing us a brand new boat and would be giving some settlements to each shipmate. Everything has turned out perfectly. Not only did we survive a harrowing experience, but we also achieved the ability to receive a brand new boat with new state of the art technology, and each mate walked away with enough money to secure his family.

My testimony is that even though we were not able to use the catch to help some of us take care of some overdue bills, God still knew what He was doing. The guy who owned the boat had insurance and his insurance paid off the whole boat and then some. He gave the guys who went out with him money for their trouble, so everyone ended up okay. God knew what the outcome would be before we even went out there. The fish that we caught was not for us. It was for the sharks that were going to attack us. God had a way of escape for us already in the works and we had no idea.

This is my life altering, faith building testimony.

Shout triumphantly to the Lord
all the earth.
Serve the Lord with gladness;
come before Him with joyful songs.

Psalm 100:1-2

FROM DARKNESS TO DESTINY

By
Tracy Elaine Thomas

On a cool November evening, as my mother, who already was a single mother of five children, began to settle into bed, I began to let her know that I was ready to enter the world. After preparing for and arriving at Mobile County General in Mobile, Alabama, I, Tracy Elaine Thomas was born.

The unique thing about my birthday is that it was also my oldest sister's fourth birthday. As my mother returned home with me, she did the best she could to take care of me and my other brothers and sisters. As I began to grow, we moved to what used to be known as Park City, Alabama. It's now known as Daphne, Alabama.

It would be at the age of six or seven when my life would forever change. This was the time where my innocence was cunningly taken away. This event would lead me into a promiscuous lifestyle of simply seeking love.

As I matured, I later became the mother of two boys who are now 23 and 25. Because the emotional aspect of my life was so screwed up, I didn't know how to love. This lead to more than one failed marriage. However, through all of this, there was something inside of me that would not let me give up.

I would be in my twenties when I learned that "something" was the Holy Spirit. It was then that God let me know that my situation would not be my destination. God decided to arm me with perseverance and determination, in spite of the fact that I was a teenage mother and a high school dropout by the age of 19.

I began to surge forward filled with hopes and dreams that, statistically speaking, I had no business having. I decided that the only way to care for myself and my two sons was to enlist in the United States Army. Before I could do that, I had to pass the GED test which took at least three to four tries. I had to earn 24 credit hours of college and I also had to pass the ASVAB entry test for the military, which I had to take twice—only to be told I had to take it a third time. I had to prove that it was me that not only passed, but raised my score by 30 points.

I enlisted in the military and stayed for a couple of years. It was at this time that I married again, only to have the man I thought would love me forever, do something that would change me forever. That marriage and separation period lasted ten years and ended in divorce.

TESTIMONY #6

25

I then made the decision to leave the country and become a government contractor in the Middle East. After being there for six months, I would meet the man that would forever change my life. God knew the type of man I needed and desired, so he designed a six-foot 1 inch tall drink of water just for me. He would use this same man to break some serious strongholds in my life. This man loved me from the very start.

One day in his office, he looked me in my eyes and told me, "All you need is for someone to love you." He was and truly is, a man after God's own heart. For the first time in my life, I knew what it felt like to be a woman. This man became and remains to be the center of my heart as my husband and friend.

My husband has made some great sacrifices to help make my dreams come true, and although I thought I would forever chase love, love was finally chasing me.

The Lord is my shepherd;
there is nothing I lack.
He lets me lie down in green pastures;
He leads beside quiet waters.
He renews my life.

Psalm 23:1-3

BIOGRAPHY OF TYRONE PINDER

By
Tyrone Pinder

I was born on June 16, 1955 in Miami, Florida. I am the only child with no brothers or sisters and I have never seen or known my father. I have completed high school and had a basketball scholarship to Florida Southern College in Lakeland, Florida. Upon graduation from college, I could not find employment, so I enlisted in the United States Army in June 1977. I was enlisted and sent to Frankfort, Germany, where I remained for four years. I was recommended to Officer Candidate School at Fort Benning, Georgia and graduated as a Second Lieutenant. I was then stationed at Fort Sill, Oklahoma and other bases in the United States. I remained in the military for about 12 years on active duty and five years in the Reserves, where I retained the rank of Lieutenant Colonel. While serving in the military, I started drinking alcohol socially and through the years, I eventually became an alcoholic.

I worked in the Atlanta Federal Penitentiary in Atlanta, Georgia from April of 1990 until August of 1999. I had to resign because I got into debt, using my pay to supply my alcohol and not being responsible enough to pay my bills. I was married for 22 years the first time I got married and I have two sons from that marriage. I got divorced and it was recommended by the Federal Court that I attend a Residential Drug Treatment Program.

Through all of this, I was a Certified Addiction Counselor, which was my position at the Federal Penitentiary. I should have known better, but I would drink after work and over a period of time, it had gotten worse. I worked at the Salvation Army from January 28, 2003 until July of 2010. I have a background in counseling, so I was given the opportunity to work in intake, counseling, later Program Director and Administrator for the Salvation Army.

Upon leaving the Salvation Army in Washington, DC, my wife and I moved back to Atlanta, Georgia. After looking daily, attending job fairs and going to employment offices, I could not find a job. I got discouraged, however, I stayed patient and spiritual. I trusted that God would make a way for me.

One day, I humbled myself to go to the VA Hospital Homeless Program and told them that I had nowhere to stay. The hospital recommended the Clifton Sanctuary Ministries and I stayed there for four weeks.

One weekend, I was getting a Marta Card at Ebenezer Baptist Church and one gentleman who was there, recognized me from the Salvation Army when I was his counselor eight years ago. He told me that he stayed at Quest 35 Transition Housing and that they might be hiring, so I contacted Quest 35 and was told to fax my resume to them.

TESTIMONY #7

Another employee that I had worked with in the past was also working there and he set up an interview for me to meet with his Program Manager. When I met her, I realized that I had known her in the past and I started volunteering at Quest 35 for about six weeks and then started working part time as a Resident Manager. This part time position would later turn into a permanent position as a Case Manager for the Veteran's Housing, which was offered to me by the CEO.

When I look back, I caused a lot of problems for myself and my family. Many times I was told that I am a very intelligent person, but my bad decisions have caused me this embarrassment. Today, I have great passion for the homeless and I like helping people because I have been there and can relate to the situation. I am an example that if you trust in God, things will work out if you listen, believe and be honest with yourself.

When I tell my story, many people look at me and tell me that by looking at me, a person would not think that I have been through so much in my life, so my passion is in helping someone who wants to be helped.

I will sing and make music to the Lord.
Lord, hear my voice when I call;
be gracious to me and answer me.

Psalm 27:7

HOW I KNOW GOD IS REAL

By
Janice Clemons

In December of 1969, while lying in my hospital bed following the birth of my second son, I had a seizure. It was the first time that this had occurred. I was treated and then released from the hospital with seizure medication. Throughout the next 20 to 25 years, I would have seizures every once in a while.

I was diagnosed with an AVM, which is an Arterial Vascular Malformation. This is a birth defect of sorts, in which the veins in my brain were undeveloped, so to speak. The neurologist who I saw, determined that I needed only to take the seizure medication and told me that I would likely have a normal life and he did not see the need to correct the malformation.

Mind you, I always thought that it was very strange that these infrequent seizures only occurred while I was asleep for the night! Incidentally, in 1985 and 1986 respectively, I lost my two older sisters due to ruptured aneurysms.

In 1991, I suffered a stroke due to bleeding in my brain caused by the AVM and this landed me in the hospital for some five-plus months. While I was in the hospital, I had nine brain surgeries to correct the abnormality that had caused me to hemorrhage. I lost the use of the left side of my body and from that time until 1999, I was wheelchair bound.

My husband did mostly everything for me during those years; brought me my toothbrush in bed, drove me everywhere I needed to go—you name it, he did it. After a while, he could no longer do for me because he had become very ill with pancreatic cancer and passed away. While my husband was ill and in the hospital, I had begun walking and leaving my wheelchair at home.

I was very determined not to be dependent upon other people to drive me everywhere I needed to go, so I started driving again. I pushed through the fear which had surfaced after not having driven for over eight years. God is able and I was willing! However, I had two accidents while becoming acclimated to being back behind the wheel again. It was quite a challenge, considering the difference in the driving patterns that I was now faced with. It was really frightening, but again, but God! I knew that I could do all things with Him!

In 2004, I began training with the American Stroke Association in preparation to participate in a fund raiser by walking in a half marathon (13.1 miles). The Lord blessed me to raise the $5,000 necessary to participate and I was blessed to complete the walk in nine-plus hours. It was the most exhilarating thing that I've ever done in my life, next to accepting the Lord in my life and giving birth to my two sons, and I praise Him, highly!

TESTIMONY #8

The Lord has allowed me to go from being independent to almost totally dependent, to where I am today, as I now live alone (that is, Jesus and me). I am now back to my activities, which include ushering and singing in a choir at church.

Oh. I need to mention that I have come to the conclusion that the seizures I had suffered with all those years, I believe, were merely a feeble attack of the enemy. HE WAS REALLY TRYING TO KILL ME! You see, I came to that conclusion recently, because on December 19, 2011, I was viciously attacked in my car, inside my garage, by my neighbor's dog, who jumped in my car as I attempted to get in and went straight to my leg and started biting it. While he was chewing on my leg, all I could do was scream for help and blow the horn, in hopes that someone, like the owner, would hear me and come to my aid, but my efforts were fruitless.

I finally screamed the name "Jesus," and was prompted to grab the dog by his collar and put him out of the car, so I did just that. Well . . . no. Correction. It was not, could not have been me. We know Who did it! Hallelujah!!!! The bottom line is that through all my tests and trials, the Lord has shown up mightily and I know that He is preparing me, and I feel better equipped to weather the storms that are sure to come . . . . with Him!

"God is our refuge and strength, a very present help in trouble." Psalms 46:1

Don't fear sudden danger
or the ruin of the wicked when it comes,
for the Lord will be your confidence
and will keep your foot from a snare.

Proverbs 3:25-26

TESTIMONY ABOUT MY ILLNESS

By
Caron Harris

Unexpectedly, in the early part of March 2011, I was awakened in the middle of the night by excruciating pain in both my back and abdomen, bringing me to tears. After being able to call my mother into my bedroom, she began to pray for me as my sister prepared to drive me to the hospital emergency room.

Upon seeing the emergency room doctor, I was told that I had a kidney stone on both the left and right side of my body. I was given a prescription for a narcotic pain medication called Lortab as well as the name of a doctor with whom I needed to schedule a follow up appointment within the next few days after my emergency room visit.

Over the next several days, I began feeling better. I even kept my hair salon appointment and planned to participate in a close friend's wedding, which was going to be held in a few days on Saturday, March 5, 2011. All went well on the day of the wedding and I did not experience any pain.

The following day however, after church service, the pain returned with a vengeance and was becoming increasingly unbearable. This time, the pain was only in the lower right pelvic area. I was unable to do any cooking and bathing proved to be very painful. Even when I was being very still, I would feel sharp, stabbing pains in my pelvic area. When I stood, I could not place my right foot flat on the floor, which was okay because not being able to place my right foot flat on the floor helped relieve some of the pain and strain.

I followed up with the urologist, who was referred to me by the hospital. After a painful pelvic exam, the doctor could not determine what was wrong with me. Since the urologist thought the pain might be related to my female organs, she wrote another prescription for Lortab and referred me to a gynecologist, who I began seeing in March 2011, and that only meant that I was to endure more painful pelvic exams.

During this time, the pain remained almost unbearable. When I would sit down, I would have to lean to the left side to take the pressure off of my right side. Many times when I would be sitting and doing nothing, I would experience intense, sharp, cramping pains, which rendered me unable to move an inch or even speak because of the tremendous pain I would experience. I would have to muscle up enough strength to call someone into my bedroom to assist me. Thank God for my praying mother, because her prayers got me through many of these episodes.

TESTIMONY #9

During my many visits to the gynecologist, I had to go through many blood tests, pelvic exams, cat scans and other types of tests; including painful vaginal ultrasounds and exploratory surgery in hopes of determining a diagnosis. While my gynecologist was performing the exploratory surgery, she had a General Surgeon assisting her in the operating room to help her in determining what was wrong with me.

The General Surgeon determined that the cause of my pain was due to an issue in the way my hernia repair surgery was done 14 years prior, so I started seeing the General Surgeon. Meanwhile, I was running out of pain medication and my gynecologist refused to prescribe any more pain medication since I was referred to the General Surgeon, even though I would have to wait before I could get an appointment. Because I could not get a prescription for more pain medication, I had to endure two to three days of unbearable pain, during which time I spent countless hours in bed and being in too much pain most of the time to even go to the bathroom.

I had Ibuprofen, but that was doing nothing to ease my pain. Once I did get in to see the General Surgeon, he prescribed a different kind of medication—patches. I would stick these patches to my skin over all the areas where I was having pain. Ha! A lot of good that did! Although I had been without pain medication for about three days, I still had pain and discomfort because the "new" pain medication was not helping me.

The General Surgeon soon determined that there was nothing he could do and because of the type of insurance I had at the time, I had to go to my Primary Care Physician, who finally prescribed me more "real" pain medication (Lortab) while subjecting me to a myriad of tests and exams. My primary care physician told me that the General Surgeon's diagnosis was incorrect and that she believed it was a lumbar (back) issue because of the fact that when I stood, I could not put my right foot flat on the ground.

So, once again, I had to go through more tests and exams while being painfully poked and prodded. When we received the test results, we learned that the diagnosis was again incorrect. My doctor tried different combinations of pain medication to try to get me off the narcotics. She even tried Gabapentin. The doctor finally determined that the only option was to send me to a pain clinic.

So, while trying to locate a pain clinic, she provided me with a referral to a neurologist, at my request. That proved to be just a bigger waste of my time and energy, and because I was now under the care of the neurologist, I could not receive any strong pain medication from my Primary Care Physician, nor could I receive any from the neurologist, because he didn't prescribe narcotics.

Finally, in August of 2011, I ended up at the Shepard Center Pain Clinic. When I first arrived there, I was not expecting too much. The doctor came in, asked a few questions, looked at me and then turned to his nurse and said, "Can you tell me what's wrong with her?" The nurse could not answer, but the doctor said he knew exactly what was causing my chronic nerve pain which seemed to spread all over my body, depending on my body's movement or lack of movement, since he had seen this before. He called it "Iliopsoas muscle pain with nerve entanglement." Finally, I received a correct diagnosis However, I would still endure three more months of chronic pain and painful therapy. During the several months of pain, I endured sharp, dull, and stabbing pain, even burning pain. There was even an episode during therapy where I begin to hold so bad I begin to feel nauseated and felt as though I would vomit.

For eight months, I was unable to work, walk, drive, or even do other simple activities around the house without unbearable pain. Combing my hair or brushing my teeth was also painful due to the nerve entanglement. Then miraculously in November 2011 after long having prayed for God to make me better before the end of the year, He did just that. I went to our church's usual monthly Women's Fellowship and as the young lady was praying for me I could feel God's power all over my body and I began to jump all over the front of that church, something I had been unable to do for the past eight months. I have been getting better and better each day ever since. Within a few days, I began to feel well enough to drive and do my hair, and soon after that, and most importantly I began feeling well enough to get a job in order to take care of my kids and myself.

When pride comes, disgrace follows
but with humility comes wisdom

Proverbs 11:2

MY STORY

By
Robert Lee

In 1985, I was at the age of 15. Mom was on dialysis and life was life. It was a Wednesday and I remember that because my mom was at dialysis that day. I rode my bike to the dialysis center to spend the day with her. Next door to the dialysis center, it just so happened to be a bike dunes. This was a place where young men came to ride their dirt bikes.

While riding my bike inside the dunes, I came upon one hole that was fifteen feet deep and the walls went up at a cold 95 degrees—practically straight up. Now, the goal was to ride the walls of this pool or hole all the way around and continue riding throughout the dunes. Well, that's where my problems began.

I had always feared this particular hole, but seen so many other young guys with less experience, ride the walls, I felt, well I can do that. So, here I go. I'm riding—I'm banking the wall side to side until I get to the drop. I drop inside the hole or pool, and I began to ride the wall. Halfway around, I did something very wrong, because I fell 15 feet down on my back and head, with the bike falling on top of me.

With every fiber in my body, I knew I was dead. I couldn't move my eyes and I couldn't turn my neck. My hands and feet were paralyzed. I even heard my head crack open. I couldn't even turn to see if there was blood. I just knew I was done.

Now, to make matters worse, where I laid placed me in the way of oncoming traffic. You see, this was an area that was highly used. There would be a bike coming through here every five seconds and I seemed I laid right in the fairway of all that traffic for hours.

During this time, not one bike came through. It was amazing, because I felt that if I wasn't dead, I was going to die real soon because someone is coming through. More time went past, which seemed like an eternity. My arms, my legs and even my fingers—nothing would move. I just began to pray. I just talked to God. I told Him, Lord, I'm not ready to go yet, but if it's Your Will, it's fine with me.

Right at that moment, I got feeling in my arms and legs and I was able to call out. There was a kid who looked down into the pool and saw me. He slid down the walls of the pool and he helped me to the top. It was truly amazing. I just knew my head was busted open and that blood would be everywhere, and I would be dead.

TESTIMONY #10

To this day, I truly believe God said No. I later found out once I made it to the top, that the reason no bikes came down through the fairway where I laid, was because right across the street was a field fire and all the kids were busy looking at the firefighters do their job.

Sometimes yo u never know how God is going to save your life and you never know who He's going to use. Well that day, He didn't magically stop the time. He didn't push a pause button and stop everyone from moving. He just simply started a brush fire—just enough for all the other kids to stop riding their bikes

Well, I'm riding back home on my bike, crying and praying the whole way, saying Thank you, Lord for carrying me through this day.

I will give You thanks with all my heart;
I will sing Your praise
before the heavenly beings,
I will bow down toward Your holy temple
and give thanks to Your name.

Psalm 138:1-2

MY TESTIMONY

By
Marc Willis

In 1997, Stephanie Willis, my sons Stepvon and Montreyll and myself, met an angel. It was a Tuesday, approximately two o'clock in the afternoon. My wife and I were going down the street of Covington Highway in the Avondale area. For those that don't know, that's Avondale, Georgia.

We came upon a red light where our vehicle had stopped. I tried to restart it and it wouldn't start. I continued to turn the key to start it and it still wouldn't start. I let it sit for a minute or two and at that time, a fire truck came and pulled up on the side of me. The officer asked, "Is there a problem?" I replied, "Yes. My car won't start." So he said, "Well, give it try now and let's see what happens."

I proceeded to start the car. The car did not start but at that same moment, smoke bellowed from beneath the car, As I tried to start the car again, more smoke came from the bottom of the car. The officer said, "Hey, hey! Stop. I believe your fuel pump has burnt out." So, they most graciously pushed the car out of the street into a nearby gas station.

One of the officers said, "Let me see what's going on." As you know, smoke and firefighters go hand in hand. He began to check underneath the car and upon his inspection he concluded and said, "God is truly watching over you all. It's a wonder you vehicle did not explode. That was your fuel pump. All the wires on the gas tank are completely burnt."

My wife and I looked at each other in astonishment. Looking at our children in the back seat, the officer said to us, "This could have been a tragedy on this day."

All we can do is just be grateful that God brought us through this situation. It truly could have been different. Well now, my wife and I had the daunting task of getting the truck repaired. Here we are, miles away from home, two babies and very little money. Well God, we need You a little bit more.

Well you see I had no money to tow the vehicle home and I had no way to bring a mechanic to me. It was a task that I would have to embark on myself. The first thing I had to do was jack the car up and drop the gas tank and pull the fuel pump out. Now, the vehicle we drove was a 1994 Ford Explorer. This was not going to be an easy thing to do. I was by myself, had very limited tools and the gas tank was full of gas.

TESTIMONY #11

Marc E. Willis

After a few moments of contemplating, I began the grueling task. It seemed that I worked on that car for three hours and in that time, I only got three bolts off. I truly didn't know what to do. The kids were crying and hungry, my wife was tired and upset, and I had the burden of all their feelings on my shoulders. As I prayed for God's help, there was a young man who was a bank teller. He had come to the gas station to get something to drink for his lunch. He asked me, "Is everything alright?" I replied, "Yes." He said, "Well, what are you doing?" I said, "My fuel pump and my gas tank burnt up and I have to repair it right here." He said, "Well, why don't you have it towed?" I said, "No money." He said, "Well, I'm taking my lunch right now, so why don't I help you pull the gas tank down?" I replied, "No, but thank you. After all, you have a suit on. You're not dressed for this type of work." He said, "Aw man, this is nothing. That's what the cleaners are for."

God knows I needed the help. I wasn't going to push him away. To make a long story short, he worked on the car until nightfall. We finally got the tank down at 8 PM that night. Not only did he not go back to work, not only did he get his white shirt messed up, not only did he give me money to feed my wife and kids, but he actually took us all home that night. But before he took us home, he took us to the grocery store. We bought food. Not only did he do that, my wife worked in Marietta. Knowing that she couldn't get to work the very next day, he offered to pick her in the morning, taking her all the way to Marietta and then take me to go work on the car.

Now, I don't know where he lived, but my home to my wife's job was approximately 45 miles, and he did all of this. Not once did he ask for any compensation. He took me to the wrecking yard the next day and I got a fuel pump. The fuel pump was $55.00 and I only had $40.00. Well—yes you guessed it. He gave me the rest.

We went back and worked on the truck all day trying to put the fuel pump in and put the gas tank back up in the truck. What we didn't finish that day, and I knew that this man had already went out of his way to help us, but my friend told me not to worry. I'll pick your wife up from work, I'll bring her home, and tomorrow I'll pick you up and we'll go get the truck fixed and get it running.

Thank God, my wife didn't have to go to work that day—it was a Saturday. Now, it's been two days and this man hasn't been back to work yet. He has become everything I needed to get this car running, and for my family to be safe. I asked him, "You think your job is going to be okay without you being there?" He said, "Aw, they'll be okay."

So, we finally got the truck running and thank God. He followed me home and the truck ran beautifully. When we got home, I asked him then. I said, "It's been three days and I've never once asked you your name." I apologized to him for that. I said, "Man, what is your name?" He said, "My name is Angel."

Me and my wife looked at each other and our mouths flew open. We had the most perplexed look that a person could ever have. We shouted, "ANGEL?" He said, "Yes." We could not believe it. We said, "No, that couldn't be your name." He said, "Yes. My name is

42

Angel." I said, "Show me some ID." There it was—right there on his Georgia State Driver's License—Angel.

I said, "Man I have to pay you for what you've done." He said, "No." I said, "There's got to be something I can do for you." He said, "Well, my brakes need to be changed. Maybe you can help me do that?" I said, "Enough said. It's done." He said, 'I'm going down to Florida Monday to my Father's house." I asked for his number and his parents number and he said ok and then he left.

A couple of days past and I called to see when would we do his breaks. When I called the number, I asked to speak to Angel. They said there was no Angel that resides there. I said, "It must be." They said no. I called his father's house and I asked for Angel and his father said, "Angel?" I said yes. He asked, "Sir, do you have the right number?" I said, "Yes. Angel is a white kid about 20 to 26 years old and about six feet tall and slender." The man said, "I know, but who are you?" I said, "My name is Marc and I live in Atlanta, Georgia.

At this same time, I'm feeling some kind of way because I can't seem to find Angel. In my frustration, I said, "Sir, do you know where I can find Angel?" He said, "Yes. That's my son." I said, "Oh ok. Do you know how I can reach him?" He said, "Well, yes and no." I said, "Well, what does that mean, sir?" He said, "Well Marc, when did you last talk to Angel?" I said, "Well, he helped me all last week." He said, "Is this some type of sick joke?" I said, "No." He said, "Well you see, Angel has been dead for three years now." I said, "Excuse me? Come again? You tell me what? He's been dead for three years? Sir, this couldn't be."

I immediately told my wife Stephanie and we just began to pray. We knew right at that moment in speaking with his father, we had been touched by an angel.

Hallelujah!
Sing to the Lord a new song

Psalm 149:1

A LESSON IN FAITH

By
Phyllis Walker

After I became a young adult and got married, I always thought that once I reached that certain plateau of being a wife and mother, I considered that I had made it. I had just gotten hired by the Federal Deposit Insurance Corporation as a legal secretary. I was finally able to pay my bills without struggling too much. I had one child at the time and my marriage was so so. My first husband was a practicing Muslim and I had felt at one time that in order for my marriage to be at its best, I needed to be the same religion as he.

I became a Muslim for a very brief period, hoping that my husband would teach me the ways of the Muslim faith. I read the Koran and did everything I was supposed to do as a Muslim wife. The problem with all of this was that my husband was not teaching me anything and he could never give me a logical reason why Muslims do what they do. I often wondered why they did not believe that Jesus is the son of God. Why did they believe that Jesus was a prophet? Why? Why? Why?

One day as I was washing my hands and face to prepare to pray, it dawned on me that I was doing something very wrong. I was raised to believe that Jesus is the son of the Living God and I was going against everything that I believed in—had always believed in since I was a child. Why was I doing this? I went to my husband and told him that I no longer wished to be Muslim. I was going back to church. Of course, he was not too happy about my decision, but he never tried to stop me, so I began to search for a church home.

My brother and my sister-in-law came over one day after they had left church and invited me to visit their church. My brother was very excited as he began to tell me how great the pastor was and how much they were learning. I said I would give it a shot and so I visited the church one Sunday with my two daughters who were 12 and 1 years old at the time. I fell in love with the church after the first visit and soon after, I joined the church. After I completed the new members class, I became a member of the choir. I felt so blessed at the time. I was learning things that were so unbelievable—things that I never heard of. It was just so amazing. My oldest daughter was involved in the Teen Ministry and my youngest was learning about God through the Children's Ministry. We were becoming one big happy family.

In one of the New Members classes, there was a discussion about tithing. I always knew about tithing from other churches that I had visited before, but it never explained to me the way that it was this night. After the class was over, I had a new understanding of what tithing was all about and I also had a renewed faith in God. I now understood that tithing was not something that was an option—it was a responsibility. It was being obedient to God's Word. I had to do it. So, after I had gotten paid, I took out my tenth from my paycheck and prepared to pay my tithes at bible study. It was a lot of money for me to put out at that time and I was really afraid to pay it. I prayed to God before I gave it and asked Him to bless me for my seed. At that time, I needed gas in my car and diapers and formula for my baby girl.

TESTIMONY #12

45

Marc E. Willis

I put my tithes in an envelope and put the money in the basket when it came around to me. After church was over, I got my girls and proceeded to the car. As I was riding out of the parking lot, I prayed to God and I said, "Lord, you said in your Word that if I tithe, you will open up the windows of Heaven. Well, I am holding you to your Word. I tithed and now I need you to keep your end of the bargain. I need gas in my car. My baby need diapers and formula. You said you would not leave me nor forsake me. Please don't forsake me now. I need your help."

Right at that moment, my Spirit was telling me to go to the ATM at the bank. I kept trying to dismiss it because I was trying to reason with that urging. Why would God have me to go to the ATM? I don't have enough money in there to get anything out, so why do You want me to go there? Even though I was nervous about that feeling, I went to the ATM anyway. I cautiously walked up to the machine and put my debit card in. I typed in my code and proceeded to check my balance. Now all the while, my mind was going back and forth. I only have about $7.00 in here. I can't take that out of the bank. This is crazy!

I waited to receive my balance. When I looked at the receipt, I nearly passed out. The paper was showing that my balance was $66.00! I did not believe that and so I went through the same steps again and again the receipt showed my balance as $66.00. After the second time, I didn't need to see the balance again. I proceeded to withdraw $60.00 from the ATM and after I got it out of the bank, I ran to the car, got in and began to cry like a baby,

I thanked God and I cried and I thanked God some more. My oldest daughter kept asking me was I alright because she had never seen me cry—not like that. My faith meter jumped 100%! I had always heard other stories of miraculous things happening to other people. I would listen, say praise God and contemplate on how good God is. Nothing I had heard would prepare me for what I experienced that night. Needless to say, I drove without hesitation to the gas station, put gas in the car and then proceeded to the grocery store, where I bought the diapers and milk that I needed for my baby. God showed up when I needed Him to and He proved to me that He is always true to His Word.

I have a renewed faith in God and a new resolve to never doubt God. I had decided that I would always tithe because I now understand that tithing is so important. If I want to be successful in my endeavors, if I want to have abundance in every area of my life, if I want to have good relationships, etc., I have to tithe. It is my obligation as a believer to do so because God commanded it. I have been on both sides of the fence. When I tithe, I can experience all the promises of God and when I don't, then I am cursed with a curse because now I am entering into a dangerous area of robbing God. I choose the side with all of God's promises attached to it. If I only do what He commands me to do, then I can truly walk in faith and hope and not worry. God will always be who He says He is. I have experienced something miraculous and wonderful and that experience will always remain close to me.

But I say to you who listen:
Love your enemies,
do what is good to those who hate you.
Bless those who curse you,
pray for those that mistreat you.

Luke 6:27-28

MY STORY

By
Yasmeen Silvera

This is a story about how God will allow you to go through something in order to teach you a hard lesson.

My story starts in the year 2008. That's the year I graduated from high school and I was so excited about starting college. I had been accepted at Fort Valley College and I was so excited. My mom made me get a summer job so that I would be able to save some money before I left for school. I couldn't wait to go to school because that meant I would be away from my mom's new husband. I did not like him very much because he treated my mom so bad. I never understood what she saw in him and why she stayed with him.

Anyway, in August, I went off to school and everything was good for a while. I made some new friends and I was doing pretty good in my classes—until I met David. David was everything I thought I wanted in a man. He was smart, funny, kind and he was studying to be an attorney. He could even recite the bible from beginning to end. Now, that seems funny but at the time, it was very impressive.

I began to spend more and more time with David. I would go to his dorm room and spend a lot of my time. My mom would always tell me that spending my time in David's dorm room was not a good idea, but of course, I was not listening.

To make a long story short, I ended up getting pregnant and had to leave school. A few years later, I tried to go back to school, but ended up getting pregnant again and now I am pregnant for a third time. This time I do have a job and I am trying to finally get myself together. I am going to purchase a car for myself when I get my income tax and I think I will finally be headed in the right direction.

I said all of that to say that through all of the bad decisions I have made in my young life, God has always been with me. I have rededicated myself to the Lord and I want to serve Him the way I was meant to serve Him. One day I will get to the point of telling David that if he does not plan to marry me soon, I will have to leave. I'm not afraid of what's on the other side, because I know that God is with me every step of the way.

TESTIMONY #13

*The one who lives under the protection
of the Most High
dwells in the shadow of the Almighty.*

Psalm 91:1

MY TESTIMONY

By
Dolores Walker

I will tell you about how God gives you peace and comfort in the face of adversity. My husband Raymond, died in 1999 from Leukemia. The disease had been in remission a few years earlier, but when he fell down some stairs in 1998, it was a turning point in his disease. Something happened when he fell that caused the disease to come out of remission and ultimately lead to his death.

I was employed as a nurse at the William Bremen Jewish Home and I worked very long hours almost every day. When my husband got sick again, I would leave work, come home and try to take care of him which was very taxing. The more sick Ray got, the more bitter he became. His doctor advised him against traveling by himself, but he would do it anyway and was totally exhausted. I always worried about him taking his business trips, but he always assured me that he was okay. I knew that he wasn't, but there was no talking him out of going on his trips.

My husband had his own architectural firm and my daughter Janis, worked for him as his assistant. I would call Jan frequently to check on my husband's well being because he would never tell me the truth about how he was feeling.

Ray finally got to the point where he could no longer work and drive as he did in the past, so he ended up in the hospital and stayed there for quite a while. I would go and sit with him at the hospital for hours on end. Sometimes I would go to the hospital, sleep over and then get up so I could go home and get ready for work. When I would talk to his doctor about his condition, he never gave me an indication that my husband would get better. I thought that it would be a good idea for me to prepare for him to die. Sometimes my oldest daughter would come and sit with Ray and that allowed me to go home to get some much needed rest. It was a really stressful time for everyone.

I thank God for giving me strength and courage during that time. I also thank Him for giving me the will to pray because I know I would not have made it if I had not prayed. I am here to tell you that if you ask you shall receive. If you ask God for something, you have to believe that it will come to past. You have to believe that you have received what you have asked God for. That goes for everything in your life. If you need peace, ask and you shall receive. If you need wisdom, ask and you shall receive. Always know that God requires something of you. If you follow the words in the Bible to the tee, you'll know what God requires of you and when you make your requests, you can bring God's promises back to his remembrance and you can expect Him to fulfill all of your needs.

TESTIMONY #14

My husband passed away quietly at my place of employment in early March of 1999 and I began the task of putting things in order. I know that God was walking with me during this time and what started out as seeming like an eternity was only for but a moment.

It has been over ten years since my husband passed. I look in awe over my life and I wonder how I got over. If it wasn't for my God . . . .

The Lord is my light and my salvation,
whom shall I fear?
The Lord is the stronghold of my life
of whom shall I be afraid?

Psalm 27:1

MY TESTIMONY

By
Cynthia Lewis

Boy! The stupid things we do for love, but now I know that God is able. My testimony begins after I had completed my first year of college at Spelman. I live in Atlanta, Georgia so I was close to school, but I had begged my father to let me stay on campus. I was involved in a lot of activities and I reasoned with my father that it would be more convenient for me to stay on campus so that I would be able to participate in the activities that I was committed to. I guess it worked because he allowed me to stay on campus.

In hindsight, that turned out not to be a good idea. I fell head over heels for a guy who was a Junior at Morehouse. He was studying to be a doctor and I really liked that about him. His name was Dewayne. From the time he ran up to me with his umbrella open to cover me from the rain as I was coming from class, I was hooked. Every single day after class, I would romp over to his dorm and that is where I would stay until I had to leave. Of course, we were having sex and I had no business in that area.

After about two or three months, Dewayne seemed to get a little tired of me and he dropped hints to me by letting me see him with other women or he would just ignore me altogether. I was not going to be outdone, so when school was out for the summer, I got a waitress job at Denny's and pretended like I was saving money for school for the next term. What I was really doing was saving money so that I could fly to the other side of world to see Dewayne.

The first time I flew to Columbus, Ohio, Dewayne met me at the airport and all was well. I enjoyed myself for the weekend and went home. The second time I flew there, I was on my own. I knew I was on my own even before then, because I took a late night flight and lied to my mother that I was going on a retreat with the church!

I got to the airport and Dewayne was nowhere to be found. I got in a cab and went to a motel where I stayed for about two weeks—I should have only been there for a couple of days, but I wanted to be around Dewayne. I got a job and decided to stay in Columbus. All this time, I was pregnant and didn't even know it yet.

To make a long story short, my mother got worried and tried to locate me. She found me and had me to go to my grandmother's house. When I got there, my grandmother took one look at me and said, "You're pregnant. We are going to the doctor tomorrow." The way that I found out I was pregnant was by the doctor coming out of her office and congratulating me and calling me "Mrs." I was six months pregnant. I didn't know this before because I was having a regular cycle every month. The rest is history.

TESTIMONY #15

God is so good that He saw fit to allow me to go through all of that to grow up. A lot of things could have happened to me while I was gallivanting around the United States in search of—on an airplane no less—on a late night flight. What the heck was I thinking? And to top that off, I lied to my mother about where I was. The ending to this could have been really tragic. What if the plane had crashed? What if there was a lay over due to some kind of malfunction with the plane that I would not have been able to explain away? So many things could have happened to me, but because God was there through all of that stupidity, I was covered and I was protected. I could have gotten to the airport and because I looked like a tourist, it could have been open season on a person like myself. I could have been raped or Dewayne might have thought I had another ulterior motive and try to harm me. I will never know what the outcome could have been, but I do know that God kept me covered through all of that. I thank God that He was with me during that time. I used to think that if we weren't doing God's will, He would leave us. God said in his word that He would never leave us nor forsake us and I believe that now.

If I had never gone through and come out of that ordeal, I would never have known the love that Jesus has for me.

I have asked one thing of the Lord;
it is what I desire:
to dwell in the house of the Lord
all the days of my life.

Psalm 27:4

MY TESTIMONY

By
Robyn Mays

On February 16, 1983 in Pomona, California, I was about to celebrate my sixteenth birthday. My parents, who loved and adored me, gave me everything I dreamed of. Most people thought I was born with a silver spoon in my mouth. My parents protected me and my brother. Life was beautiful and even more so, because I was turning sixteen today.

Today was going to be a very wonderful day for me because I was having a sweet sixteen slumber party. It was going to be just me and all of my girlfriends. It was going to be a great night tonight. There would be about 20 or more girls all coming together for me. We would talk about our boyfriends, play games and talk more about our boyfriends. At the time, there was no special guy in my life except my brother and my dad. So, I'll just have to make up someone at the party. After all, the party is all about me.

My family did a lot to prepare for this slumber party. One thing in particular, my brother had to clean up the yard, sweep up all the leaves in our courtyard, which I know he hated because he had to do it for my birthday. One of most unusual things was asked of my brother by our mother was that he get the water hose from the backyard and bring it to the front. Now it really was no reason for us to have the water hose there in the front because all of our water resources were in ground. Even if we had to wash the cars, we had a hose for that already.

So, the water hose was put in the front to make the look of the yard complete. With the yard being done and the house being prepared, the night was sure to be a blast. All of a sudden, things got crappy real fast, when my mom announced that we would have to postpone the party until tomorrow because there were some things that my mother and father had to attend to, which would mean they would be unable to chaperone the party.

So, it upset me for a moment, but I truly knew it was for the best. My brother was really hurt and upset because he would be the only guy amongst all my wonderful and adorable girlfriends. At the time, we didn't know that God was truly involved in this situation, because later that night, approximately about 2 or 3:00 in the morning during the time me and all of my party goers would have been sleep in our den where the party would have been held, there were two fire bombs thrown through the window of our home.

TESTIMONY #16

56

One hit the outside wall of the house and the other went straight through the window and landed on the area where me and my friends would have been sleeping. The whole area exploded with fire and we would have truly perished. At this time, we were in another part of the house, so the fire did not affect us at all, but we all heard the explosion.

My father ran outside and saw the fire raging. There was a sliding glass door that was locked so my father and mother grabbed some bricks and threw them through the sliding glass door and grabbed the water hose that otherwise would have never been in that spot, and with that being done, we were able to control the fire.

Firefighters soon came and extinguished the rest. It was a catastrophe. Right at that moment we knew that God was all in and about this whole situation. If the party had not been postponed, it would have been a tragedy. Now as we look back days later, we saw why my mom said bring the water hose to the front. We understand now why the party was postponed because my parents had another engagement all of a sudden. I never realized that my birthday could have become my death day along with 20 or more other girls. God was and is always and forever more remarkable in our lives. May God continue to bless us all.

I am certain that I will see
the Lord's goodness
in the land of the living

Psalm 27:13

MY TESTIMONY

By
Greg Shepard

Several years ago, I had a problem with my leg because I could not get my diabetes under control. So, I struggled an entire year trying to get my leg to heal. My doctor was concerned and told me several times that if my leg did not heal, they would have to cut my leg off.

I ended up in the hospital the beginning of the next year being told the same thing by my doctor that he had told me previously, and that was if I my leg didn't heal, I would have to get my leg cut off. I was not accepting that. I said, "No, no. God has already told me that my leg was going to heal, so my leg will not be cut off." My doctor always shrugged his shoulders and gave me the same spill every time.

Since my leg still had not yet healed, I was scheduled to go back to the hospital and have the surgery to remove my leg. I went to the hospital, but I still held fast to what my God had told me. I was not going to have to have my leg amputated. My leg was going to heal. I was holding on to that promise even though my doctor was saying something entirely different.

Now at times, I will admit that my faith wavered. There were times when I felt like giving up and I doubted God's ability, so I don't want you to think that I have always been this strong, confident person. I was really scared and I wondered if the doctor was correct in his diagnosis, so now the day had come when all that I had prayed for and all that I had hoped for would come to past. It just didn't seem that things would go, I guess, God's way.

To make matters worse, the doctor who had been seeing me and taking care of me, wouldn't be at the surgery. They had gotten another doctor who knew nothing about me to perform the amputation. I knew then that this was a done deal.

So, there I was, laying on the surgery table and feeling really groggy from the medicine that they give you right before you are given the anesthesia. I had been praying all night and I was praying now. I was praying as they were taking me from the prep room to the surgery area.

All of a sudden, my doctor, who at first was unable to make the surgery, showed up and proceeded to get scrubbed and prepared to come in the surgery area. When he came in, there was something about the atmosphere in the room. Suddenly, I heard, "Stop! Stop! Don't do anything else! We are not going to operate on him. I heard him but I was still a little groggy.

TESTIMONY #17

The nurse that was next to me asked the doctor, "Are you sure? The doctor said, "Yes, I am sure. I just believe I need to give this another check. Take him back to recovery and then take him to his room. I was taken back to recovery and then my room.

The next day, the doctor ran a series of tests. Amazingly, these tests came back showing that my leg is healing. Out of all these months being unable to walk with my foot in a cast, my leg is finally showing improvement.

Within a matter of weeks, I was truly on my way to a full recovery. Now with a few months of having physical therapy, I'm walking like Denzel Washington and soon I'll be running and popping moves like football great, Michael Vick. God is truly remarkable. I see now that trust and faith go a long way, and most of all, it endures for us even when we can't endure for ourselves.

Wait for the Lord;
be strong and courageous.
Wait for the Lord

Psalm 27:14

MY STORY

By
Trica Oxenburg

In 1993, I was a senior in high school. I was a fair student and I was a cheerleader. I was also in love with this boy, Machon. We did everything together and we really liked being around each other.

One day, we decided it was time for us to have sex, so we skipped school and we went to his house because his parents weren't home. It was my first time and it really, really hurt and I vowed I would never do it again because for something to hurt that bad, maybe I wasn't supposed to do it yet.

Well, as it turns out, my first time got me pregnant. I didn't know what to do. I told Machon and he said that I should have the baby and he would help me take care of it. I said no, because my sister had gotten pregnant a year before and my dad would have had a fit. So, I tried to hide it the best I could. I walked around the house in a robe 95% of the time and my parents didn't suspect a thing. At least I don't think they did.

One day and a few months later, my parents went out of town for a few days. No one was at home but me and my baby brother. I must have been going through labor because I got this terrible pain in my stomach and I felt like I had to go to the bathroom. I went to the bathroom and as I was sitting on the toilet, the pain got much worse. I was thinking, this is not what I think it is. Oh no!

What end up happening is that I gave birth to a 8 pound baby boy in the toilet! He was already dead and I had to get to the hospital quickly without anyone finding out what really happened. I told my brother and one of my neighbors took me to the hospital. I must have gotten there just in time because I was on the brink of death. I still had the afterbirth inside me and if that didn't come out soon, I would have died. The afterbirth is poison once you have the baby.

God is really good because if my parents had been home or I had not been able to go to the hospital, I might be memory today. God always watches over us and takes care of us even when we make dumb decisions or do stupid things.

In hindsight, I should have just told my parents and dealt with the consequences. Now, I can't have children if I wanted to because I scarred up my body so bad from the birth. I might have been dead and no one would have ever known the cause of it.

TESTIMONY #18

It's always better to tell the truth and free yourself. Whatever it is, know that God is able and He will always cover and protect you. No matter what!

Lord I turn to You.

My God, I trust in You.

Do not let me be disgraced;

do not let my enemies gloat over me.

Psalm 25:1-2

MY TESTIMONY

By
Michael Banyon
(who lives in Dallas, TX)

In 2003, I was planning to go on vacation with my family. We were flying to Los Angeles to visit my cousins for two weeks. We were really excited about the trip and talked about it every day. I had put in for time off months ahead of time because I knew this was going to be trip of a lifetime. We were planning to drive to Las Vegas to gamble and go to Disneyland and Magic Mountain. We were going to make this a wonderful two week vacation.

On the day that we were supposed to leave for the trip, my wife suddenly took ill. We didn't know what was wrong with her, so we drove to the emergency room at the hospital. I was hoping it was nothing more than gas or something like that because I didn't want to miss our flight. My wife kept apologizing to me but I was very upset. I didn't want to miss our flight because I wanted to get to Los Angeles like yesterday.

Well, as it turned out, we did miss our flight, so I called the airline to see if we could get on another flight for the next day. As I was making the phone call, we were watching television and there was news of a plane crash just after take off from the airport in Dallas. I found out later that this was the flight that we missed. It was reported that everyone on the flight was dead. It was flight 1203 leaving out of the Dallas Airport. Now, I'm not going to give the name of the airline because it would be distasteful and morally unjust for those who have family members or friends who did not survive the crash.

I dropped the phone and immediately got on my knees to thank God. If we had been on that flight, we would have been among the dead now being reported. We were not meant to be on that flight and God deterred us by causing my wife to take ill all of sudden.

God is so good! He will change things around for your good every time. When it is not your time, it is not your time. Thank God for knowing more than we could ever know. Our way is not God's way and vice versa. I continually thank God for his goodness and his mercy and I live my life to serve Him! Hallelujah!

Incidentally, my wife was fine, we were able to get on another flight and we were still able to enjoy our vacation in Los Angeles and in Las Vegas as well. We had a wonderful time!

TESTIMONY #19

Even when I go through the darkest valley,
I fear no danger,
for You are with me;
Your rod and Your staff-they comfort me.

Psalm 23:4

WHEN IT'S NOT YOUR TIME

By
Cheryl Glass

It doesn't matter what you try to do to do yourself in, when it's not your time, it's not your time. God has all of the say so over that.

I will begin my story in 1973 when I was in high school. My parents enrolled me in private Catholic School because they felt I might do better there. I wasn't a bad kid—in fact I was an honor roll student. I just liked to hang around the wrong people.

One day I had a Spanish test that I was supposed to be studying for, but because I liked to procrastinate, I didn't study and I knew I would fail. Instead of telling the teacher that I didn't study and ask for another chance to take the test, I decided that I would make myself really sick so that I could get out of taking the test.

The night before, I decided to take an entire bottle of regular aspirin. I figured if I was at least really, really sick, I would not have to take the test and my mom could come get me and take me to the hospital so that they could pump my stomach.

Well, I got really, really sick. It wasn't what I had expected, but I was still sick. My teacher thought I was joking, but I kept telling her that I needed to see the nurse and call my mother. I didn't realize that I would feel like I felt. I felt as though I wanted to be dead. It was horrible! I vomited and vomited and vomited until I couldn't do it anymore. My teacher told my mom that I wasn't really sick and that I was playing around. If I was vomiting, I doubt seriously that I would pretend to vomit. My whole insides were sore from vomiting so much. I was out of school for about a week and I guess my system was trying to get rid of all the aspirin I took.

Silly me! Looking back on all of that, I truly could have died, but God allowed me to go through that for two reasons: One—it was not my time to go and Two—it was not my time to go. No one knows when you will die or how you will die except the Father. If He is not ready for you to leave the earth and join Him in Heaven, no matter what you try to do to take yourself out, it is not going to happen.

Thank God! If I had died or seriously did harm to myself, who's to say that I would be able to be here today, alive and able to tell my story?

God is good!

TESTIMONY #20

Lord, I seek refuge in You,
never let me be disgraced.
Save me by Your righteousness.

Psalm 31:1

THE NEIGHBORLY INTRUDER

By
Anne Silvera

Last year when I living in Cleveland, Ohio with my parents, we lived in a cute little two-family house. We lived upstairs and the owners lived underneath us. The owners were pretty nice and we knew that after a certain time every night, we had to be a little more quiet because the man who lived underneath us worked at night and he needed to get some sleep before he would go to work.

One evening, my step-sisters were over for the weekend and my parents were going out. Before they left, they told us that we had to keep the noise down and we were also told not to romp around on the floor because the owner had to go to work that night. I said okay and my parents left for the evening.

Well, I guess we didn't really pay attention to what we were doing. We played, wrestled around on the floor, jumped up and down on the bed, and did pretty much anything else you would do when you are home by yourself.

We must have been making a lot of noise because all of a sudden, we all heard a lot of ramming and banging at the front door. The person at the door was yelling and cursing and he was hitting the door with a hatchet. Me and my step-sisters started screaming. We had never heard nor seen anything like before. They were telling me not to go to the door because I might get hurt.

I went up to the door. For some reason, I wasn't afraid and I asked the man why he was chopping our door in with his hatchet. He had a gun in the other hand and when I saw it, I was afraid.

"Where are your parents? Why are you kids making so much noise? I have to go to work!" My neighbor was very angry as he kept chopping the door. I said I was sorry and I said that my daddy is going to be mad when he sees the door messed up. I said I didn't know we were making so much noise but we were going to stop.

I stood by the door until my parents got home and told them what happened. I don't know what my daddy said to the man downstairs, but the next thing I knew we were moving to a new place. I also got in trouble because I went to the door. I was always told to never answer the door when they were not at home.

TESTIMONY #21

69

When I think back on that time, I know that God didn't give me a spirit of fear, but of love, power and a sound mind. I stayed calm even though it was dangerous. I am only six years old! It would have been a tragedy if that man had pulled the trigger or attacked me with the hatchet.

God always protects his children. I'm a living witness to that.

Rejoice in the Lord, you righteous ones;
praise from the upright is beautiful.

Psalm 33:1

Glory be to God!

For the word of the Lord is right,
and all His work is trustworthy.

Psalm 33:4

A TESTIMONY BY

Bishop Hin

In the early 90's, in the city of Chicago, I was a ramp agent for Continental Airlines. The actual job I did was to retrieve baggage from the baggage compartment of the aircraft. In other words, load and de-load the plane with luggage.

On this particular day, there was a storm brewing in the city. The flight had already been deplaned with passengers, but the luggage was still on the plane, due to an electrical storm that was taking place at the time.

Now, it is the policy of the airport that in any electrical storm, all ramp personnel are not to be in any open areas or around the aircraft where electricity can travel through the plane and electrocute an employee.

You see, planes are big, giant magnets for electricity. So, we knew that the passengers were waiting in the baggage claim area for their bags, but the luggage was still on the plane. Our supervisor, despite the orders that came down from airport administration to stay out of the weather, mandated that we go and retrieve the luggage from the plane. We did this knowing that something was going to happen.

As I was putting bags into the tug to drive them to baggage claim, I felt a sharp tug on my arm. Before I knew it, I was laying on the ground still conscious and not able to feel any parts of my body except for the rain hitting my face and a burning sensation in the center of my back.

I didn't quite know what was happening. Before I knew it, that was it. Now before I go any further, I can only tell you what fellow employees told me. My shoes were blown off of my feet. They were cut up and burnt up. I was dragged under the shelter out of the storm. Individuals that grabbed me said that I was burning up. I was so hot, that they could barely stand to hold me. If you didn't guess by now, I was struck by lightening.

The paramedics were called as well as the doctor from the hospital infirmary. I was pronounced dead at 4:30 pm. I'm told I laid there on the ground until the paramedics placed my body on a gurney and at that time, there was an investigation going on. Forty-five minutes to an hour later, a coroner arrived to retrieve my body.

They put me in a bag which zipped up, and placed me inside of the vehicle. Apparently, I was on my way to the morgue. Now, I can't tell you how long it was between them putting me into the coroner's vehicle and the time God performed His miracle, but now, this is when I came to.

TESTIMONY #23

While in the coroner's vehicle, I awakened to total blackness. I slowly realized that I was trapped inside of something and I started to panic. I began to scream and move, not knowing that I was in a big coroner's body bag.

During the same time I was panicking, I hear voices and I hear screams. It was the drivers. They looked back and I guess they tried to stop the vehicle, but they jumped out without putting the car in park. The car went over and crashed in a small ravine, where it came to rest at the bottom. I smelled smoke and gas. I began to tear my way out of this body bag.

As I began to tear myself out, there were people helping me and pulling me out. I didn't know at the time what had happened. I only remember being at the airport. I noticed that my clothes were soaking wet and I didn't have shoes on my feet. My feet were blistered very badly with burns, as well as my fingers. I went to the hospital.

While at the hospital, police, doctors, new crews and more came. I was then told that I was struck by lightening at work. I was pronounced dead at 4:30 pm there, and on the way to the morgue, I came back alive inside the body bag, some one hour and 45 minutes later.

My fiance' at the time and I were floored. I knew then that Christ held the papers to my life. I can only do one thing from this day forward—preach a very strong and faith-based message throughout the world. Now I will say that there were many lawsuits through all of that, and let's just say I now know what electricity can do and what a lawsuit can do when you sue the airline, the airport, the paramedics and the coroner's office.

I have built one of Milwaukee's largest churches and shelters for the homeless. I thank God that He truly gave me a second chance.

He loves righteousness and justice;
the earth is full of the Lord's unfailing love.

Psalm 33:5

I WAS MEANT TO BE

by
Shawna Wilson

I was born December 8, 1959 and I almost didn't make it. You see, I was my mother's first child and the way in which I was positioned in the womb was a strange one. I was a breach baby, which meant that I was positioned feet first. The doctors tried to turn me around manually and as hard as they tried, they couldn't get me to turn around.

In the 50's, medicine was not as advanced as it today, so there was only so many things a doctor could do to make sure that the baby could come out without danger to any of the baby's organs. They almost opted to perform a Cesarian on my mother, but it was too late in the game. I was ready to be born then. Also, there was the risk that I would not make it and the danger was just as serious for my mother.

The only option left to them was to try to pull me out by my feet with forceps. The new danger with that was most of my nerves in my head could be severed and I would end up with serious mental complications.

Well, the forceps worked and some of my nerves in the top of my head were severed, but thank God, there was no serious damage. The nerve endings grew back together and I have grown to be a functional and vibrant young woman of 53.

My testimony is that God allowed the doctors to pull me out into the world with forceps and the damage was minimal and temporary. God has a purpose for my life and thank God that he has allowed me to be here, live a blessed life and do his will for my life.

TESTIMONY #24

I will praise the Lord at all times;
His praise will always be on my lips.

Psalm 34:1

THE TESTIMONY
OF KEVIN DURHAM

(Posthumously)

When Kevin found out that he had kidney failure and had to be on dialysis, he was not very happy about it nor did he accept the fact that he would have to go to a clinic three days a week to go through a grueling dialysis treatment for three or four hours.

When he first got to the dialysis clinic, he was not friendly. He was mean and nasty; he barked and growled at anyone who dared to speak to him. He was a very unpleasant and unhappy individual with a very bad attitude. He was a person who was dealing with a lot of demons from his past and his present.

Kevin had been on dialysis for many years, first with the VA Hospital and later with the Davita Clinics. His attitude about God and life in general was really taking a turn for the worse. The nurses, the doctors and even his fellow patients at the clinic did not want to deal with him.

One day, it was decided that Kevin would be sent to an "Attitude Adjustment" facility for a month, in hopes that he would come out of it a better person. Well, as it turned out, Kevin did come back to the clinic a totally different person with a totally different attitude.

When he returned to the clinic after undergoing his attitude adjustment, it appeared that Kevin was a different person. He was smiling, which was odd because no one had ever seen Kevin smile. He apologized to some of the patients for his previous behavior and he now had a renewed love and appreciation for God.

Kevin learned from his experience at the facility that there was someone who cared about him and what he was going through and that someone was God. He now knew what love was; how to give it and how to receive it.

During Kevin's last days and weeks of his life, he often reminisced on what he could have done better and how he wished he had known God before. He was so thankful for the opportunity to know God and to love Him and he was finally at peace with himself and he was also finally at peace with God.

TESTIMONY #25

I waited patiently for the Lord,
and He turned to me and heard my cry for help.

Psalm 40:1

A TEST OF TOUGH LOVE

by
Brittany Omstead

When I was in the 11th grade, I became pregnant by my boyfriend. The worst thing about was that I had to tell my mother. I was really afraid to tell my mom but when I finally told her I was pregnant, she was okay with it.

My pregnancy went okay and my mom helped as much as she could. I gave birth to a healthy baby boy and everything went well—for a while. I began thinking that since I had a baby, I was grown and I could do anything I wanted. I was in control of my life because I just gave birth.

My mom had made me go back to school to get my diploma instead of just getting a GED. My mom thought that just getting the GED was a sign of being weak and that I could go back to school, take the classes and graduate from high school and get my diploma, so I did that.

I guess my arrogance must have taken its toll because the day that I came home with my baby and my mom saw that the baby had no shoes on and no coat on and it was very cold outside, she was upset. When she asked me why my son was dressed like that, all I could say was, "You can't tell me what to do. I don't have to listen to you!"

What in the world did I say that for? My mom just stopped in her tracks and politely said, "Ok. Since I can't tell you what to do, I want you to get out my house now. Leave the baby, and don't get nothing that you didn't buy and get out now."

From that day forward, I had the roughest time. I had a rough time with my pregnancy. I had to stay with my boyfriend in his mother's house. The only reason she let me stay was because I was pregnant. I was very angry with my mom for putting me out and I always called her to ask if I could come home. She always said no.

My testimony is that despite the fact that I was disrespectful to my mom when she tried to help me and despite the fact that I was resentful toward my mom, I know my mom was right in what she did. God only knows what type of person I would have been if she disregarded my remark and did nothing. I appreciate the fact that she made me leave the house. I learned from that experience and I grew up. I had to learn to become an adult and a parent. At first I wasn't ready to be a parent and I had to learn the hard way. I know I took my mom through a lot of problems, but I love and appreciate her now more today than ever. I thank God for my mom and I thank my mom for showing me—tough love.

TESTIMONY #26

Happy is the one who cares for the poor;
the Lord will save him in a day of adversity.

Psalm 41:1

THE DOG WHO SAVED MY LIFE

by
Elaine Johnson

One day, I was driving home from the grocery store and I was kind of in a hurry. I was trying to get home so that I could begin preparing dinner for my family. I was in such a hurry that I didn't see the dog that was just standing in the street. As I was coming around a curve, I attempted to swerve so as to not hit the dog and because I was so close to the curb as I swerved, the front of my car hit the curb and my car flipped over.

I found myself upside down in my car in shock, very disoriented and in pain. What I didn't realize at the time was that my arm had been severed from my body. I slowly worked my way out of my wrecked car and proceeded to go somewhere—anywhere so that I could get some help for myself.

As I started walking, I still did not realize that my arm was missing. I was losing blood fast, but I couldn't stop until I was able to use someone's phone or at least get to the hospital. The last thing I remember before I passed out was making it to someone's home and knocking on the door.

I was told later that I was found collapsed at the front door of someone's home, my arm missing and blood everywhere. I was rushed to the hospital where doctors tried desperately to stop the bleeding. The performed emergency surgery on me and when I woke up, I was in a recovery room with a cast on my arm and tubes in my arm and nose. God is a good God! I could have died right there on that person's front door, but because people acted swiftly, my life was saved.

When my car crashed and flipped over on that curb, I didn't feel my arm separate from shoulder. I knew I needed to try to get out of the car and find help. I was successful in missing the dog and it's a good thing I was. That dog had to be an angel—a messenger from God. The dog obviously was sniffing around the car looking for whatever it is that dogs look for and he found my arm. The dog probably thought it was a very large bone or something and he promptly took it to his home where he probably would have buried it.

A neighbor happened to notice the dog carrying something very large in its mouth walking casually down the street and took the object from the dog. When the person saw that it looked like a human arm, it was taken down to the police station. I guess the person thought that someone may have been murdered or hurt or something and maybe the police could do something with it. Well, it turns out that the police called the hospital to find out if someone had come in that day missing an arm—you know the rest of the story.

If it had not been for that dog, who knows? I thank God that He uses any person or any animal to fulfill His promises and to fulfill His purpose. I very well may have been missing an arm today and having to learn to do things without the benefit of having two arms. I could have been paralyzed or something worse. I could have died.

TESTIMONY #27

82

What the devil wants for your bad, God will surely turn it around for your good! I thought my life was going to take a major turn for the worse, but God made sure that it didn't happen.

God is our refuge and strength,
a helper who is always found
in times of trouble.

Psalm 46:1

MY INSTANT MIRACLE

By
Angela Davis

Miracles happen when you don't expect them to, that's a fact. I'm a living witness to that. God does not work in the way that you expect him to. In fact, God truly works in mysterious ways and lot of times His ways don't make sense to us. Maybe they are not supposed to make sense.

I used to be employed by the FDIC (Federal Deposit Insurance Corporation). I did really well on my job and I enjoyed it immensely. I was living in an apartment complex with my youngest daughter. I did everything I could to make sure that all my bills were paid, my car was taken care of and that we had enough food to eat. For the most part, I was able to accomplish those things. I was going to church on a regular basis and I was also a member of my church choir.

One day, I received a phone call from a collection agency telling me that I owed $250.00 on a bill that was very past due. I was also told that if I didn't have that money into their office by 6:00pm on the following Friday, they would garnish my check.

Now, I had never gotten a call like that before and it really upset me. I could not be garnished or else I would be fired. The FDIC was very strict on things like that. I prayed that night and asked God to work out that situation because I had no idea how I could come up with that much money in a short period of time. Later that night, I had a dream where I was at a party and a strange lady came up to me and said, "Your number for today is 886." The dream was so real and so vivid, I thought it was actually going on. When I woke up, I remembered the number.

All day long, I felt a tugging at my spirit telling me not to forget to play these three numbers on the Cash 3 Lottery game. Now, I had never played the lottery and I wondered if it was God telling me to do this or the devil. All day long, I kept feeling like I had butterflies in my stomach—like I was anxious for something. When I left work to go home, I still felt that urging, "Don't forget to play those numbers on Cash 3."

Well, you know, I did play 886 before I got home and while I putting the numbers on the sheet to give to the cashier, the butterfly feeling was even stronger. I called my sister, who was living with me at the time, and I told her to make sure the TV was on Channel 2. I rushed in the house and sat right in front of the television as I waited for the announcer to pull up the three balls in the machine. I was very excited and afraid at the same time, but I felt like I did the right thing by playing the numbers.

As the announcer was calling off the numbers, I followed along. "The first number is 8. The second number is 8. The third number is 6. Tonight's numbers for Cash 3 are 886." I couldn't believe it. I screamed and hollered and screamed some more. My sister thought I had lost my mind. "I won! I won! Oh Praise God! I Won!"

TESTIMONY #28

I immediately turned and got back into my car so that I could cash in my ticket. I had won exactly what I needed to send to the creditor! God is good! For Real!

I cashed the ticket in and got a money order for $250.00 and immediately sent it off to pay the creditor. That was one bill I never had to worry about again.

That's what I mean when I say that God works in ways that we might not understand and now I know that sometimes we are not supposed to understand His ways. Now, I'm not saying that God condones gambling or the lottery, but what I am saying is that God works in mysterious ways, His wonders to perform. We are to just listen to our spirit and follow it exactly. God will never let you down. He will never leave you nor forsake you. God is a Good God!

This is my testimony.

Be gracious to me, God,
according to Your faithful love.

Psalm 51:1

SOMETHING
THAT MAKE YOU GO, HMMM

My name is Cassie Arnold and this is my testimony and if I were to give this a title, it would be **SOMETHING THAT MAKES YOU GO HMMM.**

Oh, the silly and stupid things that we do when we are young! The good thing is that once you come to know Christ Jesus, you know longer do stupid and silly things because you have now learned and understand the ways of Jesus and you now follow Him. You no longer drink the milk of babies, but eat the meat of truth, wisdom and righteousness.

When I was about 21 or 22 years old, I was a married woman with a child. My husband and I were having financial problems at the time and I asked my mother to keep my daughter for a little while until we got things together. I had a nice shape, long hair, beautiful eyes and a gorgeous smile (at least that's what I have been told). As I walking to the train station one day after getting off from work, a car passed me that had two guys in it. The car stopped, backed up and one of the guys asked if I wanted a ride home. I hesitated for a second and toyed with the idea of getting in that car with them. If I accepted a ride from them, would they really take me home or would they take me somewhere and rape me, or worse, kill me?

My curiosity really got the best of me and I accepted the ride. As I was giving directions to where I lived, the guy that was driving said, "Hey. Do you mind if we make a little stop first. I promise I will take you home right after, okay?" What was I going to say? I was already in the car. He drove me to this nice condo in the downtown area and he asked me to come in. I went inside and admired the way this guy had his place decorated.

It started getting late and I told the guy that I really needed to get home. As I said before, I was married at the time. The guy kept reassuring me that he would take me home, but I knew he had other things on his mind. He invited me to come and look out of his window with him, which I did. As I was looking at the view, he started undoing the buttons on my blouse. I moved away and really insisted that we go.

To make a long story short, both of those guys had their way with me. It was not very pleasant and I felt horrible. If my husband had only known what I was doing at the time. I was supposed to be at home and I knew that he was there waiting for me and wondering where I was.

Thanks be to God that my life was spared! The guy did take me home after they did what they wanted to do and I asked them to let me out at the corner of my street so that it would look like I just got off the bus. My mother had always taught me not to accept rides from people that I didn't know. How stupid of me to play Russian roulette with my life.

TESTIMONY #29

I could have been killed—God gave me mercy. I could have contracted some type of disease and given it to my husband—God saved me. I could have been beaten up and left for dead somewhere—God gave me grace. God has always protected me from danger and from myself. I thank the Lord now and forever for being my great protector. I love the Lord!

I am at rest in God alone;
my salvation comes from Him.

Psalm 62:1

TESTIMONY OF
FARRAH SILVERA

My name is Farrah and I'm from Chicago, IL. I know that God is a protector. I know that God will keep us from all harm and danger. I know these things because about fours months ago, my mother, her husband and I were living in an apartment on the south side of Chicago. I was preparing to leave for college in about one month.

My step-father had gotten sick and my mother took him to the hospital. They were at the hospital for most of the night and I was so sure that they would keep him and my mother would be at the hospital with him all night. This is the moment when all of my foolish thoughts, foolish ways and ignorance began to subdue me, because I invited my next door neighbor over to spend some time with me—not to mention, he was a married man with two children, all living right next door. While he was over, we engaged in a lot of foolishness and I knew that my mom had taught me so much better than this, but all those things she taught held no weight to all the hurt and loneliness I felt inside.

To compile my problems even more, my mother and step-father came home, and what do you know? I still had this guy in my room. Yeah, you guessed it—it gets even worse. You see, my parents like to sleep in the living room and as fate would have it, the front door was on the other side of the living room and we were in a high-rise apartment complex. No jumping out of windows allowed. Now, I was stuck with this man in my room the whole night. I had never been so nervous and scared in my life. If I wanted to do something at that time, I couldn't. The only thing I could do was pray.

I think if God had a way of getting my attention, He finally had it. My mother even came into my room during the night and didn't even notice that this guy was in the room. Talk about holding your breath. I figured that I could sneak him out once they went to sleep, but as fate would have it again, they stayed up talking and looking at TV the whole night long.

Well, I knew that my mom and my step-dad had to go to work the next morning and that would be my way of escape. All's well that ends well. So, the morning comes and as luck would have it, my step father was off from work. You know, my mom always said that what you do in the dark will always come to the light and she also would say something about those bones in the closet, but I don't remember that exactly, but this situation has truly changed my life.

I just had to "woman up," and make ready to my step-father to what's about to go down. Before I could pull myself to go and tell my step-dad that there is a man in my room and he's trying to go home, but you stand between him and the door. So, my step-dad says to me, "Bring him out." Before I could say anything to my friend, he comes out the room anyhow, ranting about how badly he needs to get home to his family, because he hasn't been home all night. I was so embarrassed, hurt and most of all, ashamed.

TESTIMONY #30

After the guy left, my step-father and I talked and I didn't want him to tell my mom and he didn't want to tell her either, but he said there were some things he could withhold from my mom, but this was not one of those things. He said for him not to say anything to my mom would be hindering the blessing that would come to me. I guess you could say that there's lessons in this that will teach us all.

I called my mom and I told her what happened and she was very disappointed in me. I sat and thought about the beating I was going to receive from this, but I quickly realized that the beating wouldn't be half as bad as the one that God was giving me at that moment. You see, I never felt so low and used.

My mother told me to go to my room and stay and when she gets home she would deal with me. I realize today that God's grace is sufficient. His mercy is everlasting and that it all endures through the most deadening of times. You see, I could have contracted any type of disease, not to mention AIDS. His wife could have found out where he was at all night and come over and do harm to me or my family. So many bad things could have come from this, all because I allowed Satan to set up residency in my temple.

I thank God that now I can look back on this and know that through all of the blocks and the walls that were put up in my trying to get this man out of this house, I know that God is still in control. I didn't see no way out of this, but I heard my momma say that if God saw you to it, He will bring you through it.

This is my testimony.

Farrah in Chicago, IL

We give thanks to You, God;
we give thanks to You, for your name is near.

Psalm 75:1

ONE of My Testimonies

I have really, really learned to TRUST in God. I have been blessed all of my life to have everything that I wanted. From an early life, my parents were able to give me all of the necessities and then some. When I say that I have always had everything I wanted, I truly mean everything. My parents bought my first car the day after I got my driver's license at the age of 16. After that they bought the next 4 cars for me. Well, I have always thanked God for my parents and my parents for teaching me about God at an early age.

Although, I have always had a personal relationship with God, I never had to test my faith because whenever I needed emotional or financial help I could go to my parents. I am reminded of a time when I was well into adulthood and I made a stupid choice, and did something that could have landed me in jail. Several people at my job told me about how they were able to get a new car and get their current car paid off and take several thousand off the cost of the new car. Well, I bought into the scheme sink, line and hooker. I went to the dealership and picked out the car that I wanted with all of the bells and whistles and the Holy Spirit condemned me right away and I knew that I should not go through with the scheme. The salesman that I was working with was the person running the scheme. After I picked out my car, I went back to the salesman's office and he started the paperwork. He then told me that I needed to write a check for $10,000 and that he would give it back to me before the deal was sent to the lender and no one would ever find out. I tried to back out and then he proceeded to show me a stack of checks that he had collected from his other customers. He said, "this is a foolproof plan", that I have created over time and have never gotten caught". As I wrote a check for $10,000, my stomach dropped because I knew that this was against the law and more importantly a sin. The enemy was telling me that it really wasn't wrong because I would be making payments and that the car was over-priced anyway. Yes, I drove off in my beautiful new car and had the other one paid off and my new payments would only be $150.00.

A couple of weeks later, while on vacation visiting my parents I checked my voice mail at work and had a message from the dealership asking when they could deposit my check for $10,000. I immediately called the salesman and was told that he no longer worked for the dealership. I called his cell phone and of course there was no answer. I didn't know what to do. For the rest of my vacation, I worried about what was going to happen to me. My Father asked me what was wrong and I broke down and started crying. I told him what happened and he could not believe that I had done something so stupid. He told me to go back to the dealership and tell them what I did and ask for my "old" car back. When it was time for me to return home, my parents took me to the airport and didn't mention anything about my dilemma. As I was boarding the plane, my Mother handed me what appeared to be a letter and told me to open it once I got home. When I got home, I opened the letter a cashier's check for $10, 000 fell out. I immediately called home and thanked my parents profusely. I finally got on my knees and asked the Lord for forgiveness and asked him to be with me when I went to the dealership to face the music. Do you notice that I didn't mention going to God before? It wasn't that I didn't have a personal relationship with him, but I didn't know how to pray to ask him to get me out of this mess that I had created. So you see I have always been able to go to my parents for all of my needs and wants. Well, that all changed in 2007, when both of my parents passed away.

TESTIMONY #31

I have been unemployed for 2 years now and I have had to really test my faith and depend on God. I was receiving unemployment and it was stopped abruptly in Sept of 2012. All of my bills were due and I had cut off notices for EVERYTHING! I prayed and said that I was not going to worry about it because I remember my Pastor saying, "If you are going to Pray, don't worry. If you are going to worry, don't pray". As I prayed to the Lord, I said that I didn't want to ask anyone for anything because I believed in his word. It was so hard to not ask anyone for help, but I continued to pray and I didn't mention my situation to anyone. Well, just at the most crucial time I got a money order in the mail for $1,000.00 from an anonymous sender. When I opened the letter, I dropped to my knees and started thanking God for his faithfulness. It was not so much the money, but that he was teaching me who my Provider is. He is truly Jehovah Jirah! This is a life altering, faith building testimony.

Cheryl Kelly

An Ambassador for Jesus Christ

How lovely is Your dwelling place,
Lord of Hosts.

Psalm 84:1

THE LITTLE THINGS
THAT GOD DOES

One of the little things that God does is allow women like Bertha Lewis to live a full life to the ripe young age of ninety-one years old. Bertha was born in 1918. She was four feet and 11 inches tall. She raised five children—3 girls and two boys. The oldest is 75 years old today and the youngest is 56 years old. She worked hard all of her life and was attentive to all of her children and most importantly, she was a God-fearing woman. "Little Miss Five-by-Five" was her nickname. When she dressed up, she was the sharpest woman on the block. She always wore the best clothes, wore the best shoes and most of the time, had the best of everything. One of the things that Bertha was most remembered for, was the fact that she always, always, always talked to Lord. She had her own personal relationship with the Lord.

One of the little things that God does is allow women like Dolores Lewis to grow up, get married, raise four children two years apart, become a Licensed Practical Nurse and then a Registered Nurse and then on to become the Director of Assisted Living at a Jewish Home in the Atlanta, Georgia area. When her husband was diagnosed with Leukemia, she remained tirelessly by his side until his death in March of 1999. Realizing that she could no longer remain in the home that she and her husband shared for many years, Dolores searched for and found an apartment where she now lives along with her youngest daughter. Dolores has been through a hysterectomy, two hip surgeries and a back surgery and through it all, she has come through a trooper. Many people who meet Dolores for the first time, often think that she is younger than she really is. For a 75 year old, she really does look good. God has truly blessed her. One thing that Dolores always says is that "You have to trust in God. I know first hand. If I didn't trust God, I would not have been able to get through the tough road that was before me after my husband died. That's why you have to pray and trust in God." Obviously, "Dee" knows what she is talking about.

One of the little things that God does is allow a woman named Betty Bowers to bear the death of her only son to the likes of a motorcycle—something that she was much against her son getting involved with. She was always afraid that he would get hurt or something worse. Well, the something worse happened, but God kept her and made her stronger. Her faith was made stronger because of her son's death. God allowed Betty to survive a double mastectomy and a knee surgery and she moves around better than a 23 year old woman. Betty is 78 years old and a retiree of AT&T. She and her husband have run many businesses together and have been very successful in them. God has surely been good to Ms. Betty because he has been a provider, a healer and a protector in her life.

TESTIMONIES 32, 33, 34

The one who lives under the protection
of the Most High dwells in the shadow of the Almighty.

Psalm 91:1

THE LITTLE THINGS
THAT GOD DOES

One of the little things that God does is protect and keep his children. One day, as a little boy was driving a combine through a wheat field on his family's farm, one of the blades on the combine got stuck. He got off the combine to try to unloosen the blade and as he was trying to do this, the blade moved forward and cut off the boy's arm. The boy was conscious enough to pick up the severed arm and walk the whole distance of the wheat field until he was able to get to his home, where he collapsed on his front porch. His father found him and promptly rushed him to the hospital where the doctors were able to reattach his arm. God protected and kept that little boy until he was able to get to the hospital.

One of the little things that God does is to give us those men and women who become doctors and nurses and scientists to help save lives. These sensitive and caring people are always working tirelessly to find cures for diseases and developing medicine to help others live long and productive lives.

One of the little things that God does is to prevent a hard-headed little boy who has been told repeatedly not to mow the lawn in his slippers, from getting his toes cut off while doing just what his father warned him not to do. The boy was mowing the front lawn with his slippers on and his father had always told him not to do this because of the danger of the mower blades rolling back and doing damage. When the boy had finished mowing the lawn, he was putting the mower up and the blades were in motion. While his feet were close the mower, the blades rotated backward and cut the top of his slipper straight off. If his toes had been in the same area that was cut by the mower, he would have been missing all five of his toes! That boy was saved from a possible horrifying experience. That's one of the little things that God does.

TESTIMONIES 35, 36, 37

Lord, you have been our refuge
in every generation

Psalm 90:1

INCEST

by
Anon

When my brother and I were younger, we were very, very close. We played together, talked a lot with each other and most of all, I think we respected one another's point of view. I was always my brother's keeper—literally. When some kid in school would try to bully him because he was a quiet person who kept to himself, I would play the protective big sister and put that kid in his or her place. I was never afraid to fight, even though I was never the one who started the fight. I was fiercely protective of my brother and for that matter, all of my siblings.

My testimony in this is that God gave mercy and grace to my brother and I in that time of ignorance. Because of our little experiment, it really could have turned into something worse—like me getting pregnant! Imagine the turn our lives would have taken if we had an inkling of what we doing and really ended up having sex for real? I don't even want to think about me having to tell my parents that I was pregnant—by my brother! Oh my God!

The saying that often comes to mind and one that I have always heard my mother and my grandmother say is, "God takes care of babies and fools." How foolish to even think about one of my family members in a sexual way. That's why God destroyed Sodom and Gomorrah. The foolish things that go through one's mind. When children are not taught the way that they should go, they go any way they can go. Every time I think about that time, I thank God for his protection of me and my brother. We were certainly foolish, but we were just young kids. Even though we are not accountable for the things we don't know or acknowledge at the time, we become accountable when we come face to face with the truth.

I thank God for giving us the Holy Spirit. This is my testimony.

TESTIMONY #38

The Lord reigns! He is robed in majesty;
The Lord is robed, enveloped in strength.
The world is firmly established;
it cannot be shaken.

Psalm 93:1

TESTIMONY

By
Elizabeth Gardner

My name is Elizabeth Gardner and this is my testimony. About 2 years ago in 2011, when I was on spring break in Florida, I attended a birthday party that was for someone from one of the local colleges in that area. It was held at a local hotel on the 10th floor.

When I got there, the party was really going well. There were a lot of people there and everyone was either getting high or drunk, but for the most part, I was having a good time. I danced some, smoked a little weed, drank a little wine (well more than a little) and then some.

I got rather tipsy and stumbling around a little and for that matter, so was everyone else. Now, it's right around this part that I am not sure what actually happened. All I know is that as I was stumbling around, I lost my balance and fell right into the 10th floor window. I thought the window was strong enough to withstand a lot of pressure, so at first I didn't worry about it.

When I hit the window after stumbling into it, it broke and to my surprise, I went right through it and began to fall ten stories down to the pavement. As I was falling, I still couldn't believe that I actually went through the window. I was screaming hysterically and whatever high I had been under, suddenly went away. I was sobering up very fast.

I don't remember hitting the pavement. I don't remember anybody trying to perform CPR on me and I don't remember the ambulance coming. When I did wake up, I do remember the pain that was all over my body. I had broken almost every bone in my body.

Later I was told that everyone thought for sure that I had died. Someone tried to perform CPR and then the ambulance came. The paramedics performed CPR and they were successful in resuscitating me.

To make a long story short, after 6 surgeries, lots of physical therapy and a lot of time, I am still here. I was told that I may not walk ever again, that I had lost a lot of my brain functions and that I would have problems for the rest of my life.

My testimony is that despite all of the odds, I am still alive. God has seen fit to allow me to live for a purpose. I am a walking, talking miracle and it is through Jesus Christ that I am able to tell my story. I came back from a brief period of being dead to a much longer period of being alive, to being able to live life to the fullest and to start over.

TESTIMONY #39

When I fell through that 10th story window, I was supposed to be dead, but God wanted me to have life and have it more abundantly. If God is for you, who can be against you?

I will probably have to go through physical therapy for the rest of my life, but through Christ, I can do anything. This is truly my life altering, faith building testimony.

Shout triumphantly to the Lord,
all the earth.

Psalm 100:1

THE TESTIMONY OF RENEE WARE

Philadelphia, PA

This is my testimony. In 1981, I had just started working for the FDIC in the Legal Department. At the same time that I got hired, I also had quite a few bills that needed to be paid, but I had no way to pay them.

I had befriended one of my co-workers and we always ate lunch together. One day at lunch, I had been worrying about my finances so much, I broke down and started crying. My friend asked what was wrong and I just told her all about my financial troubles.

My friend said, "Wow Renee. I wish I could help you. Then she most graciously said, "Wait a minute. What if I got a loan for you? Would that help you?" I said, "yes that would help me but that's too much. No, you don't have to do that."

I didn't know what to say! I was so happy that someone wanted to help me, I became overwhelmed and cried some more. My friend insisted on giving me the help and she had only one requirement—and that was to make sure that I pay the loan back for her and I was more than happy to oblige. What a blessing!

Needless to say, I got the loan and I paid off most of my bills and the ones I couldn't pay off, I paid them up enough to make the balance more manageable. I paid the loan payments every month on time and my friend never had to ask me about the payments or anything.

I thank God that someone cared enough about my situation to want to bless me. My friend blessed me so that I could be a blessing to somebody else. I thank God for that chance because it does feel good.

Since my friend has blessed me, I was able to pay my bills and get them caught up. Since I have been blessed by her, I in turn have blessed others with money and my time without giving it a second thought. If it had not been for my friends' assistance and faith in me, I would not have been able to return the favor through the love of Jesus Christ.

I want to thank God and thank my friend for showing me mercy and kindness in the face of adversity. This is my faith building, life altering testimony.

TESTIMONY #40

Serve the Lord with gladness;
come before Him with joyful songs.

Psalm 100:2

OBEDIENCE

By
Jobie Collins

My name is Jobie Collins from Cleveland, Ohio and this is my testimony. When I was a little girl growing up in Cleveland, I always tried to listen to my mom and do everything she told me to do. I didn't talk to strangers and I went straight to school and straight home everyday like my mom had taught me to do. Because I was obedient to my parents, I had a stress free, problem free childhood for the most part. Most of my nonsense came about when I became a teenager, but that's another testimony in itself.

On one particular winter day, I was leaving the house to go to school. That day started out like any other cold, wintery day. I kissed my mom goodbye and left out of the door. The ground was very icy, which meant that it was also very slippery—and cold.

I walked very carefully down the steps and went to the sidewalk to begin the short walk to school. As I was crossing the street, I heard a loud screeching coming from my right. When I turned to look and see what the noise was, I was hit in my side by a car—yes—the car that was making the loud screeching noise.

I fell to the ground hard and I heard this voice saying, "Little girl! Little girl! Are you alright?" I couldn't answer because I was in pain. My whole body hit the cold, icy ground. I had ice and snow in my boots, all through my gloves to my hands, in my hair and any other place that wasn't covered up. As the man came closer to me, I tried to get up so that I could run. My leg was hurt really bad, but it didn't matter. All I was thinking about was my mom saying to me, "Don't ever talk to strangers."

Even though my leg was hurt really, really bad, I got up and ran as fast I could back to my house. I was crying and yelling for my mother. The man who hit was running right behind me. "Wait little girl! Are you okay? Are you okay?" Just as I was running up the steps to my house with this intoxicated man following me, I fell—not like when you fall to the floor if you slip on something. I fell up the steps. I fell so hard that my breath was taken away. The edge of the steps went into my diaphragm. From the moment I fell into the steps, I couldn't breath. I kept gasping for air like someone just tried to strangle me. Before I knew it, the drunk man was at the front door. My mom ran downstairs. "Jobie, are you okay? What's wrong?" "I can't breath, mom! This man hit me with his car and when he tried to talk to me, I ran!"

TESTIMONY #41

My leg was really throbbing now and my mom wanted to take me to the hospital. The man at the door was trying to explain what happened. He was very intoxicated and had not been paying attention when he was driving down the cold, slippery street. He even offered to pay my doctor's bill. My mom told the man that he didn't have to pay anything. "I've always told my daughter to never talk to strangers, and I'm glad that she listened to me."

My leg was starting to hurt worse. I knew I needed to go to the hospital, but I wanted to go to school instead. You know, God knows the plans He has for us. I told my mom that I would be okay and darted out the door. I didn't want to be late for school and my leg was getting worse by the minute. It was also turning purple now and becoming increasingly more difficult to walk on it. I must have forgotten that it was very icy and as I was running trying not to be late for school, I slipped and fell again. I decided that I would just go back home and let my mom take me to the hospital. I'm glad she did because when the doctor saw my leg, he actually thought that one of my parents had tried to beat me.

By this time, my leg was swollen, black and blue and I couldn't walk on it. My testimony is a simple one. I thank Jesus that I was obedient to my mom. I can only imagine what would have happened if I got in that man's car. I did say he was intoxicated. You could smell the beer on his breath a mile away. Jesus saved me from that man because only He knows what might have happened or what he had on his mind that day. I have always heard the saying, obedience is better than sacrifice. I now know what that means.

This is my life altering, faith building testimony.

Hallelujah!
Give thanks to the Lord
for He is good
His faithful love endures forever.

Psalm 106:1

TESTIMONY OF EUNICE BROWN

My name is Eunice Brown from Cleveland, Ohio and I am a cancer survivor. I never thought in a million years that I would end up battling this deadly disease, but I did and my faith is much deeper and stronger because of it.

I had always been a healthy person. I ate right and I took very good care of my body. I didn't smoke, I didn't drink, and I made sure that I went for a mammogram screening every year. I was very successful with my real estate business and life was good.

One day when I had just finished taking a shower, I went through the exercises of checking my breasts for any lumps or anything else that felt strange and my worst fears were realized. I did have a lump under my left breast. I was wondering how the lump seemed to get there overnight. I didn't feel this yesterday, I thought to myself. I called my doctor to make an appointment and the receptionist heard the urgency in my voice so she asked me if I was able to come later that day. I told her yes and she made the appointment.

When I got to the doctor's office, I was so nervous that my clothes were sweaty, my head was sweaty—pretty much every single part of my body was sweaty. My doctor reassured me that everything would be fine. First, the doctor's assistant had an X-ray done and after that, there were other tests done. I was told to call the office in a few days for the test results.

Well, as it turned out, I didn't get the chance to call. My doctor called me and asked me to come into her office. When she said that, I knew that it couldn't be good news. I found out later that day that the lump I felt in my breast was malignant and it would require some aggressive therapy to get things under control.

My heart dropped to my stomach. Cancer? How in the world did that happen? I didn't think cancer was something that ran in our family. I knew my sister's husband had leukemia and my dad became ill because of liver cancer. I just never thought I would get it. My doctor reassured me that the type of therapy she wanted to try would probably do the trick. We just had to try it and have faith.

Have faith? Was she serious? So, I began to go through the therapy. Twice a month, I went to my doctor's office to go through chemotherapy. I hated it! I really got sick and I always felt terrible. I was trying to endure, it was very hard to do. I started to wonder if God was punishing me for something that I was not aware of or something that I did in my past.

TESTIMONY #42

I went through the chemo for several months and it seemed like each time I had a treatment, I would get worse. It did not seem as though I was going to beat this thing. I think that during that time, I prayed more than I had ever prayed before. In fact, I believe that everyone in my family was praying a lot more. There were a few scriptures that I held on to during this time that I still hold on to today.

The most important one was God will never leave me nor forsake me, and if God is for you then who can be against you? There were a few more, but these were my staples.

After about six or seven months of chemo, the doctor did another X-ray and some more tests. This time, she did not find anything. Nothing at all. It's just like Jesus was giving me another chance.

This is my faith building, life altering testimony.

Who can declare the Lord's mighty acts
or proclaim all the praise due Him?

Psalm 106:2

TESTIMONY OF
CRAIG STEWART

My name is Craig Stewart from New Orleans, Louisiana and this is my testimony. My wife Lisa and I had been trying to have a child for a very long time. Lisa would go to the doctor and have countless tests done and I would do the same. Each time that we thought there was a little ray of hope, we were let down. Lisa's doctor finally told us that we would just have to keep trying. There was nothing wrong with Lisa and there was nothing wrong with me. So, we just relaxed a little and carried on with our lives.

About a year later, Lisa came home from work and she was crying. When I asked her what was wrong, she reassured me that her tears were tears of joy. We were going to have a baby in about nine months! I was speechless. I too began crying. We were both so happy because finally our prayers had been answered.

We both immediately started preparing for the pregnancy. She started eating better and I made sure that I was taking care of our home as well as building a nursery for our new addition to the family. Everything was going fine and then suddenly, our lives got turned upside down.

Hurricane Katrina! That storm was so devastating. Our home was completely destroyed. We were both home when the storm hit and we didn't have time to get out. My wife was hurt very badly, but the only thing she was concerned about was the baby. The Red Cross was in New Orleans and they came to help us. We got food and clothing and my wife received some medical attention. She was hurt so bad that the doctors had little hope of her surviving. At that point, she was only concerned about her baby. She had already given the baby a name—Grace.

My wife started having contractions and the doctors decided that they would take the baby. My wife would not survive because her injuries were so extensive, but the little one would be given a chance. A emergency C-Section was done and little Grace came out alive and kicking. My wife Lisa, was not so lucky. She died soon after giving birth. I am thankful to God that she did get to see her baby before she died.

So, here I was alone. I was a widower with a small child. I slowly began to pick up the pieces and moved to Atlanta to live with relatives and find a job. After all, I needed to be able to care for my new baby and myself.

Because of my "Grace," God opened doors for me that I never thought would be opened. I have raised a good, God-fearing child. Grace will be attending college soon and she will study to be a doctor. I'm very proud of her.

TESTIMONY #43

Marc E. Willis

I am reminded of a portion from Psalms 23: Surely goodness and mercy shall follow me all the days of my life. I can add Grace in there also. Surely goodness, mercy and Grace shall follow me all the days of my life and I shall dwell in the house of the Lord forever.

My daughter has been my rock. I always talk to her about her mother and the older she gets, the more she reminds me of my sweet wife, Lisa. Lisa would have been proud of our daughter.

Grace abounds!

This is my life altering, faith building testimony.

Yet He saved them because of His name,
to make His power known.

Psalm 106:8

The Testimony of Bishop Paul A. Pittman

My life began on June 2, 1971. I was the second son of two children born to Bishop David and Pastor Linda G. Pittman. I was born in Atlanta, GA. From birth my adversity began. My mother carried me for eight months and was told that if she were to just bump into anything it would instantly kill me. At the age of 10 was the beginning of impure thoughts that would lead to a suicide attempt. Did you hear what I said? At the age of 10. The devil knows long before you get here the plans God has for you and because you are so anointed, he can't harm you so he put it in you to harm yourself.

I tried the suicide attempt, only to hear an inner voice that was so loud I thought that others, if they were present would've heard it. As I got ready to pull the trigger, this voice loudly said "DO YOURSELF NO HARM! GOD HAS WORK FOR YOU! Upon obeying that voice, something in me woke up to the fact that our GOD chose to invest his purpose into such a young fragile vessel.

At the age 16 of viciously attacked by a family member who stabbed with a flat headed screwdriver and beaten with a baseball bat. When it was asked why they did it, the reply was "he made me mad".

By the age of 19, I was getting married and just knew that It would be an almost storybook wedding but I was wrong—So wrong. While working on my car outside of my apartment building, my one stand jack was shaken by an unexpected wind. The entire car falls on my chest and collapsed my lungs. All my breath was in my throat. A mysterious man with bare feet pull me from under the car, and walked away. My elderly neighbor saw him. I went immediately behind him to thank him but he was gone. No name, no voice, just walked away and never seen again. Two days later that same elderly woman died and from her death bed she told her daughter, "I saw an angel"

At age of 21, I was robbed while waiting for a on a bus. I had two dollars in my pocket. The robber stepped back and looked at me, and pulled the trigger. The gun wouldn't go off. He tried a second and third time. The gun wouldn't go off. He backed up and ran. He turned around and fired the gun, and it went off. God's grace prevailed again!

By the time I was 22, I received a doctor's report that I was sick with pancreatic cancer and didn't have very long to live. I was down to 98 lbs. I had irritated bowel syndrome so that no food could stay in me. No liquid, no anything. My grandfather said "y'all come and see Paul now . . . he is not gonna make it". People came around looking at me as though I was laying in a casket already. In the mist of it all, GOD spoke to me and said "do you wanna live?" . . . . i replied "yes!" He said "then get up and live" . . . I replied but I can't eat anything, but he told me to eat anyway. The food stayed down . . . GOD literally brought me back from the dead . . . I am elated and grateful for all that he has done.

If you trust in the Lord and step out on faith, he will not make you look foolish . . .

TESTIMONY #44

Happy is the man who fears the Lord,
taking great delight in His commands.

Psalm 112:1

TESTIMONY OF VINCENT MOTO PHILADELPHIA, PA

My name is Vincent Moto from Philadelphia, PA and this is my testimony. Several years ago, I was wrongfully convicted of rape. The woman who claimed I had raped her did not even know me. I didn't even know her, but because this woman claimed that I raped her, I was arrested and I spent 101/2 years in prison for a crime that I didn't commit.

How could this be? I had a pretty good childhood. I went to the best schools and came from a loving family. Everything just changed for me in a twinkling of an eye. No one wanted to hear what I had to say and as far as the police, the courts and the jail was concerned, I was nothing. I was lower than dirt. There was no way to prove my innocence. No way at all. I felt less than a man and I became very agitated.

Any guy you talk to in jail will always tell you the same thing about a crime that they are accused of—they didn't do it. In my case, it was really true. I didn't do it. I was really innocent. At the time that I became incarcerated, there was no DNA testing. If a DNA test had been done in my case, I never would have gone to jail. But God is good!

In 1987, my case became the first case in the history of Philadelphia to use DNA testing to prove a person's innocence. After I was found innocent of the rape charge, I wanted my record expunged. Of course, the court denied my request and I was told I would have to pay over six thousand dollars ($6,000) to have my record expunged. Why in the world would I pay such an exorbitant amount of money, especially since I did not rape anybody? I fought very hard to get the DNA testing—10 years worth of fighting. I had been incarcerated since 1977! Almost my whole life was caught up in a system that cared less if was guilty or not.

When the results of the DNA came back, it was discovered that this woman who accused me of rape was a married woman and they found four different sperm samples, from four different men and none of those men were me. I'll say it again—God is good! I would have not known about DNA testing at all had it not been for the prodding of a fellow inmate who urged me to watch The Phil Donahue Show in 1987. He had several former inmates on his show. They were free because of DNA testing. They like myself, were innocent of their crimes and DNA testing was the vehicle to prove their innocence. The guest on the show said that there are many people in jail who are innocent of crimes and their innocence could be proven through DNA testing. I then wrote a five page letter to Phil Donahue explaining my situation and the rest is history. Mr. Donahue forwarded my letter to the guests who were on the show and they took my case, which lead to my release.

TESTIMONY #45

I thank God that He allowed me to stay sane throughout the whole ordeal. I thank Him for keeping my family safe while I was in jail and I thank Him for giving me a new purpose in my life.

If I never had God in my life during that time, I don't know what I would have become. I'm stronger today because of it. It is still very hard for me because people in general don't view you as innocent. All they know is that I was in jail for a crime, I must have deserved it and that's that. It never occurs to people that a person just may be innocent of the crime that they are accused of. I was caught up in a very bad circumstance, but I was delivered never to return to that part of my life. All I can do now is pick up the pieces and try to make a life for myself and for my children. Picking up the pieces is hard when you try to complete an application for employment and you have to tell the prospective employer that you were convicted of crime and you spent some time in jail. There is no space to write, yes I was convicted, but I was innocent. I have become an advocate for those who are wrongfully accused of crimes and I work very closely with other former inmates who have experienced the same type of mistreatment as I have. Because of my experience, it has helped me to become a better father and a better man.

God is truly a good God! He will fight your battles for you and you will be victorious as long as you have faith and trust in the Lord.

This is my life altering, faith building testimony.

Hallelujah!
I will praise the Lord with
all my heart

Psalm 111:1

THE TESTIMONY
OF NICK YARIS
Philadelphia, PA

My name is Nick Yaris from Philadelphia, PA and this is my testimony. My testimony begins in 1982. At that time, I was convicted of rape and murder and was sentenced to die. I spent 23 years on Death Row and solitary confinement. I was in a prison in Huntington, PA that was condemned by the United Nations for its practices of torture, and for two years I was not allowed to speak. Can you imagine not being able to talk for two years? Because of DNA testing, my innocence was proven and I was released from prison after being there for 23 years. I give all thanks to God, the Father.

I believe that I am one of the most strongest people that God has ever created. I say this because of all that I endured in prison, I had come to know and understand that it didn't matter what other people thought of me. It didn't matter if they thought I was innocent or guilty. What mattered was that I knew I was innocent and I held on to that for the 23 years that I was incarcerated and on death row.

Nowadays, I really enjoy being outside in the fresh air and I think that is where I will be. I was locked up for such a long time, I get paranoid being indoors for a long time. I don't like it and I feel very uncomfortable. Since I have been released from prison, I have become active with an organization called The Pennsylvania Abolitionists Against the Death Penalty. When I was incarcerated, I corresponded quite frequently with this organization. It was reassuring to know that there were people on the outside who were fighting the cause for people like me. It was just the natural order of things for me to return the favor by getting involved with them once I got out. It is because of people like Jeff Garty and others who fought for my life, that I decided that I would return the favor when I was free. These people have my total respect.

When I was in prison, I became a fighter and a believer. My faith was tested every single day that I was incarcerated. There were those who cared less whether I was innocent or not, people who tried to destroy evidence that could set me free, the inmates themselves who tried to break my spirit. I had to keep fighting despite all of this. My spirit could not be broken.

TESTIMONY #46

One of the many things I have learned is this. Being found innocent entitles you to nothing. If I had been released from prison on parole, I would have more rights and more benefits than I do now. Paroles are entitled to health care, job placement, a place to live, etc. If you are found innocent, society says, oh well, you're innocent and so what?

All I received for my trouble was $5.00—yes $5.00 from the state of Pennsylvania and they set me free. All I know is this: God is everything. Family is everything. Without God there is nothing. This is my life altering, faith building testimony.

All that He does is
splendid and majestic;
His righteousness endures forever.

Psalm 111:3

THE TESTIMONY OF WILTON DEDGE FLORIDA

My name is Wilton Dedge from Florida and this is my testimony. My story starts out very similar to those you may heard already. I was incarcerated for 22 years in the Florida State Pen. In 1984, I was convicted of rape and sentenced to two life sentences. I have known inmates at the prison that were convicted of much greater crimes and they didn't get sentenced to two life sentences! It is so hard to believe that 22 years of my life are just gone—missed.

It was not until I got in touch with an organization called, "The Innocence Project," that things began to turn around for me. Through the Innocence Project, I received pro Bono assistance from attorneys who really took an interest in my well-being and genuinely wanted to see me released from prison. The District Attorney who was instrumental in my conviction in 1984, has tried very hard to prevent me from going back to court.

I went through DNA testing and the results concluded beyond a shadow of a doubt that I was innocent. It seemed that the only people who wanted to see me get out of jail was my family and my attorney.

If it had not been for God, and for the Innocence Project, which I believe was sent to me as a gift from God, I would still be in prison today. God will open doors for you when it seems that all others are closed. He will truly make a way out of no way. I am a true believer in the power of Almighty God.

This is my life altering, faith building testimony

TESTIMONY #47

The works of His hands are
truth and justice;
all His instructions are trustworthy.

Psalm 111:7

TESTIMONY OF
LISA BROWNING

My name is Lisa Browning and my permanent address is the Ohio Reformatory for Women in Marysville, Ohio. I am currently serving a life sentence for 12 counts of murder and robbery. I have been here since I was 16 years old and by the time I am up for parole, I will probably be dead. First, let me start by saying at this time, I am 30 years old and I have been incarcerated for 15 years now. I have truly come to know and understand my guilt in the crimes I have committed. I'm not writing this for show nor sympathy. I'm writing this because during my incarceration, I have discovered through my crimes that the lives I cowardly took, belonged to Jesus Christ, my Lord and Savior and their lives were not mine to take. I will be up for parole in the year 2097.

I grew up in a nice home, with good parents and friends but I thought I wanted and needed more. I never felt like I could express myself or talk about my problems to my parents because it was unheard of. As long as I didn't have a life threatening disease or pregnant, I was okay—but I wasn't. I never felt loved enough and I was always looking for someone or something to make me happy.

I started hanging out with the wrong crowd and there all my troubles began. I met a guy who seemed at the time, the perfect man. He was my Prince Charming. He told me he loved me and treated me the way that I thought I should be treated. Now, I knew right from wrong and my boyfriend would ask me to do things that I knew went against everything that I was taught, but because I thought I was in love, I did whatever he asked. He was my world.

My life began to go down very fast. I started skipping school when before I was your typical straight A student. A lot of times I would stay out late or not go home at all. During the Christmas weekend of 1993, I would participate in several events that would change my life forever.

I had run away from home and had not been home in three weeks. My boyfriend and I were bored and out of money, so we thought of different ways to get some money. We spent the whole weekend robbing and killing people with no regard for what we were doing. By the time the weekend was over, we had murdered six people, injured two people and had less than $50.00 that we had taken—and for what?

By the time it was all said and done, my boyfriend went to prison and was on death row, another girl who was with us and myself received life sentences, never to see the light of day. I have the rest of my life to think about what I have done and I truly regret it every single day—not because

TESTIMONY #48

I'm doing time and not because I'm tucked away from my friends and family, but because the lives I took, they would never have the chance or the opportunity to even experience this much. I know and understand now that just to open my eyes in the morning and breathe God's fresh air each day, is by itself, one of God's most valuable, valuable blessings. My boyfriend was sentenced to death in 2006 by lethal injection and sometimes I think that should have been my plight.

I was crying out of help, but I really didn't know how to ask for it. I was a confused little girl and I got myself involved in something that I truly knew nothing about. I ask the Lord for forgiveness everyday. I get to sit in prison and live and the lives of the people that I took will never be able to carry on.

There is nothing I can say to the families that I hurt, and their lives are changed forever because of what I have done. If I can say anything to them, it would be that I am truly sorry. I am not the same person that I was so many years ago and if I would have just looked to the Lord from whence cometh my help, my life would be so different today.

If you are reading this testimony, I want to let you know that your strength cometh from the Lord. The devil can only do to you what you allow him to do. Don't allow the devil to take control over your life. Look to Jesus. He will truly set you free!

This is my testimony.

In loving memory of all the victims and their families who suffered needlessly by my hands.

*The fear of the
Lord is the beginning of wisdom;
all who follow His instructions
have good insight.
His praise endures forever.*

Psalm 111:10

TESTIMONY OF
DEE DEE AND STACY

My name is Dee Dee. I am an inmate at the Women's Super Max Prison in the State of Ohio. I was arrested at the age of 18 for aggravated robbery and felonious assault. I am now 20 years old and I have already served two years of a 9 year sentence.

Since I have been incarcerated, I understand that I am in here because of myself. I can't blame anyone for this one. I'm in jail because I made the wrong choice—the wrong decision. but God works in mysterious ways!

All the crimes that I have committed in my young life were done because I thought I needed an outlet. You see, I didn't have a father or a father figure. My mother and I had no relationship and for many days and nights, she or I were not around one another enough to love, learn or honor anyone or ourselves. I never thought about what kind of harm I was doing to the people I victimized and vandalized. I just did the crime.

I didn't have anyone to love me or care about me, so therefore crime became my witness. If I could steal it, I did. If I could shoot it, I would. As far as killing, it only seemed to be a matter of lime. While incarcerated, God quickly brought me closer to my crossroad. I never imagined out of all the years I have been in jail and all the senseless crimes I committed, that I would come face to face, with an inmate that looked, walked and talked like me. I soon came to wrap my arms around her and embrace her—but God had a plan, and I'm starting to see His plan unfold.

You see, the lady that I've come to love and hold is my mother. She was convicted of drug trafficking and she was sentenced to three years. A mother who I've never seen, never held nor ever loved is now all that I speak about. It is so like god to allow so much to go down and the and outcome of it all be more that I could ever bargain for. I understand that my testimony has many twists and turns, but the one thing I do understand is that God's promises are true. He'll never leave your nor forsake you. For the first time in my life, I can see my life being altered, my faith being built like none before.

This is my testimony.

To all those that I victimized, I'm sorry that I cannot replace what has been taken, but it's all I have to offer.

TESTIMONY #49

Give thanks to the Lord,
for He is good.

Psalm 118:1

TESTIMONY OF CHERYL KELLY

My name is Cheryl Kelly from Atlanta, Georgia and this is my testimony. I own a small photography business that I have been asking God to assist me with. I do all types of photography and I am very good at it.

One day, I received a call from an up and coming recording artist who wanted me to accompany her to a gathering at a nightclub to take pictures of her for her CD. Now, I have not been to a club in years and I was questioning God as to whether I should attend this affair or not. This can't be what God would have me to go. For what? What could I possibly benefit from attending an affair at a club—especially to take pictures for a secular artist? I had no idea what God's plan was for me that night.

I prayed about it and then decided to go. I gathered my photography equipment and went to the club. I'll tell you this—I felt like a fish out of water. I did not fit it. I didn't belong there.

As I was sitting along at a table, listening to the music and observing the people there, a gentleman came and sat down. He looked very upset and was crying. I asked him what was wrong and he told me that he was really worried about his mother and he really didn't want to perform that night. As he was telling me about his mother, I suddenly felt compelled to pray with him and so I asked him if I could pray with him. He agreed.

We prayed very fervently and he thanked me profusely afterward. He told me that he felt much better and that he knew at that moment that everything would be alright with his mother. The gentleman then proceeded to go up on stage, pick up his instrument and said, "I'm going to do things a little different tonight. Thanks to a young lady that prayed with me, I want to offer my thanks to the Lord." He then started playing, "Yes Jesus Loves Me" right there on the stage.

To my surprise, everyone in the club stopped dancing and joined with the man as he was singing the song. It was very, very moving.

My testimony is that even though I felt out of place and weird about going to this club, God wanted me there because there was something for me to do. I was supposed to be there as an ambassador for Christ! I was supposed to be there to give a word to someone who really needed to hear it. God used me as a vehicle for His message to be heard! I praise God for that. He really does work in mysterious ways, His wonders to perform!

This is my life altering, faith building testimony.

TESTIMONY #50

Whom have I in heaven but you? And earth has nothing I desire
besides you. My flesh and my heart may fail,
but God is the strength of my heart and my portion forever.

Psalm 73:25-26 NIV

LIFE IS BOTH
AN ADJECTIVE AND A NOUN

By
Bill Lyons

The dictionary definition of life is the animate existence or period of animate existence of an individual. A noun. It also can mean the mode or manner of existence.

I have been a hemodialysis patient for over a year and a half now. I was accustomed to traveling the world and enjoying a full life. I thought all of that would change when I started dialysis. I was ambulatory and in a wheelchair, and I thought the life I once lived was over. The reality of kidney failure is that life will change, but with the proper diet and exercise, you can still enjoy a full life. I am no longer in a wheelchair. I am riding my bike and traveling again. I pay very close attention to my diet and take my binders regularly. I am not only living, but enjoying a full life again.

TESTIMONY #51

THE TESTIMONY OF JONE WILKERSON

JONAH IN THE BELLY OF THE WHALE

My name is Jone Wilkerson and I am 65 years old. This is my testimony.

Last year, six of us were on a fishing trawler, fishing off the coast of Northern California and we were out there trying to catch some fish. A lot of us were depending on this catch to help us pay up on some bills. Some of the fisherman were really behind, so this particular fishing trip meant a lot.

On that day, the sea began to produce gale-forced winds. The waters were so rugged that the entire crew felt that it would be best to turn about and bring the boat back into shore. This was to be a very important fishing haul. You see, we had a goal of two tons of fish to catch, and that was a goal that we desperately needed to reach. The waves of the ocean began to batter the boat extremely hard, and the crew and I felt that it wouldn't be long until the water began to enter our vessel. We still had a feeling of hope because after all, we were on a strong built boat and we also had state of the art safety equipment for this sort of thing. We had a water pump to safety take the water out of the boat before it became too dangerous. We came upon a large school of fish and threw the nets out to catch them. I never saw so many fish in all my life. All the nets were full and the crew was really happy.

At this time, the boat began to take on water. We were advised to turn up the water pumps full speed. In fact, the boat was taking on so much water, that the boat began to tilt as if it was going to turn over. The water was very rough and we were really having a tough time keeping the water from filling up the boat. It was starting to sink fast from all of the water in it.

Because the boat was tilting so, it was very hard for me to keep my balance and I slipped and fell toward the anchor. I hit the anchor so hard that my leg was impaled by the hook of the anchor. I was in a lot of pain and I was bleeding quite a bit. All of a sudden I thought of another danger. There were sharks in the water and all they had to do was to smell my blood and it might be all over for me.

Well, as I had guessed, the sharks were smelling my blood and it was more than one shark coming our way. By this time we were in the water and we had to get out of it. Someone radioed the Coast Guard and they were on their way with helicopters. In the meantime, we had to figure out what to do about those sharks.

TESTIMONY #51

Well, that large school of fish that we caught was still on the boat, so what we did was let that catch go back into the water, nets and all. The sharks attention was turned away from us and their attention went to the fish, which they ate. I mean they ate every bit of fish that was in that net! I guess they were pretty full, because a few of them came our direction, but they didn't bother us. That was a blessing!

The Coast Guard did finally come and they aided us in getting out of the water. After all, we didn't want to wait for the sharks to get hungry again. I was taken to the hospital so that my leg could be mended and a couple of the other crew members were there to have a doctor look at their scrapes and cuts. It was really an interesting day.

After all had been said and done, we had lost a $95,000.00 boat. We had lost approximately $300,000.00 in fish and equipment and all five guys, including the captain down to the youngest mate, survived with just cuts and bruises. We were relieved to be on board a rescue ship on our way home.

Weeks later, the captain informed us that the insurance company would be purchasing us a brand new boat and would be giving some settlements to each shipmate. Everything has turned out perfectly. Not only did we survive a harrowing experience, but we also achieved the ability to receive a brand new boat with new state of the art technology, and each mate walked away with enough money to secure his family.

My testimony is that even though we were not able to use the catch to help some of us take care of some overdue bills, God still knew what He was doing. The guy who owned the boat had insurance and his insurance paid off the whole boat and then some. He gave the guys who went out with him money for their trouble, so everyone ended up okay. God knew what the outcome would be before we even went out there. The fish that we caught was not for us. It was for the sharks that were going to attack us. God had a way of escape for us already in the works and we had no idea.

This is my life altering, faith building testimony.

The Lord is my strength and my shield; my heart trusted in him,
and I am helped: therefore my heart greatly rejoiceth;
and with my song will I praise him.

Psalm 28:7

MY TESTIMONY

By
Joy Rivers

I had a conversation with a very close friend. Since we have known each other since we were babies, we conversed about past times—which was not any different from previous discussions. However, there was one thing that was not the norm. After touching on the topic of Faith and trusting in God, our conversation seemed to linger there. We talked about MY life. Now, I am usually not one to talk about myself since I am more of a listener. However, I was reminded that my life has been filled with innumerable highs and some extreme lows. The twists and turns happened so quickly. Let me explain . . . .

I was born and raised in Trenton, New Jersey. Family, friends and church were my life; I loved every bit of my upbringing. However, at the age of 19, my life took a drastic turn . . . my MOTHER passed away of cancer. This was also during my freshman year of college. Therefore, I had to withdraw from college and go through the unbelievable process of living without the person I loved the most—my mother. Not only did I withdraw from college . . . I subconsciously began to withdraw from life. I believe this was my way of surviving. I did not want to 'feel' anything anymore. This zombie-like state was how I went through the motions day to day. For a time, I was completely out of my element. People may not have known this, but this was my internal reality. All in all, Jesus became a 'tangible' friend. Although I could not see or touch Him, His supernatural presence was enough to hold me and He continues to fill the void. He was preparing me for what was to come.

Let me fast-forward to 2007. In 2007, I was convinced that I must've been something special because the devil tried his best to take me out both mentally and spiritually. In a nutshell, the following happened: My paternal GRANDMOTHER passed away in January '07; my HUSBAND unexpectedly passed away in his sleep in May '07 (and our son was only seven months old); my FATHER was hurt in a hit-and-run accident (June '07) in which he suffered severe brain damage . . . and I'm still in my right mind only by the grace of our God! He's a keeper; I'm reminded of this fact every time I look at my son and my reflection in the mirror. I know that God is STILL preparing me for what is to come! Even though I do not understand, I am expecting God to blow my mind! In the meantime, I will continue to be faithful to Him and His perfect will.

It took a conversation with my close friend to remind me that JESUS is the epitome of a friend. You will not find another like Him. Here it is . . . the year 2012 . . . and our Heavenly Father has been with my family and me through it ALL. What a FRIEND we have in Jesus!

Joy Findley Rivers

TESTIMONY #52

Make haste, O God, to deliver me; make haste to help me, O Lord.

Psalm 70:1

PREFACE

The following testimony and biography describes Ms. Andreka Eberhart, who is an MS survivor as well the co-author of this book.

As you will soon read, Andreka Eberhart is a woman who has beat the odds. The odds that she would live to see another day was very slim, but she made it. About 9 years ago on September 8, 2003, when Ms. Eberhart was diagnosed with Progressive Multiple Sclerosis, she was given little chance of survival.

With prayer, the love of family and friends, and changing her diet, Andreka has returned stronger than before. Andreka Eberhart is a true testimony to the miracles that God can perform. Her story is a powerful one and is filled with faith and love for Christ.

Enjoy!

ANDREKA EBERHART'S STORY

Missy (MS) My Girlfriend For Life

When people hear the words, Multiple Sclerosis, they panic; and with good reason. There is no cure for MS, no miracle drug, no established program for recovery. Seven years ago when I passed out behind the wheel of my car, I should not have survived. I should have become the next statistic on Atlanta's dangerous interstates. Instead, I miraculously survived and was rushed to the hospital where a team of doctors tried to figure out what was wrong with me.

My strange symptoms began in the winter of 2003. Right after I had oral surgery, I started to lose the feeling in my legs and began dropping things for no apparent reason. My symptoms got worse and that summer I went to the Emergency Room because I was having balance problems. The doctor said I had an inner ear infection. After that, I accidently ran over a dog because I was starting to have vision problems. That August, I was a bridesmaid in my cousin's wedding and passed out at the front of the church just as my cousin started to walk down the aisle. That was the First of two times in one week.

Days later, after I passed out behind the wheel of my car, I finally realized I had to stop pretending. This was serious. The Emergency Room physician who examined me confirmed my fears when he told me he suspected Cancer, Tumors or MS. I cried as terror paralyzed me. How could this be happening to me? I wondered. I was told that I would be admitted to the hospital on the IICU neurological floor. Why was God punishing me? I was told I needed a spinal tap and brain biopsy to be sure. I was terrified and begged God to find another way.

The next day the doctor came in and told me that God had heard my prayer. He said he would not have to perform a spinal tap to make the diagnosis, he would only have to perform a few MRIs on my brain and spine. I wept with relief and the alternate procedure was done. After a few days, the Neurologist came in with a diagnosis. September 8 2003 He said that I had Severe Progressive Multiple Sclerosis. He said the lesions on my brain were hard and they had been there for ten yrs. I was only in my twenties at the time. I was release from Northside Hospital and transferred to Shephard Spinal Center MS institute for inpatient rehab.

Multiple Sclerosis (MS) is a disease that is characterized by loss of myelin knows as demyelization. Myelin coats the nerve fibers and is composed of fats and proteins. It serves as insulation and permits efficient nerve fiber conduction. In MS, demyelization usually affects the white matter in the brain, but sometimes it extends into the gray matter. When myelin is damaged, nerve cell death may occur resulting in impaired bodily functions resulting in numbness and eventually paralysis and blindness. Every case of MS is different. For some people, the symptoms are mild. For others, they can be more severe. Specific symptoms such as fatigue, depression, and vertigo are standard. Other symptoms can include Numbness in the arms or legs, Pain, Loss of vision, Muscle weakness or tremors, Paralysis, Vertigo, Fatigue, Difficulty with speech, Bladder dysfunction, Depression, Hearing loss, and Itching.

I felt like my oxygen supply had been cut off when he told me there was no cure. As I tried to process through the news, I found myself wishing I had not survived the crash. I had been given a death sentence. The treatment plan only included medication designed to stall the progression and pain. I reminded God how I always tried to take care of my body. Then God reminded me how I wanted to know my purpose before I was 30 years old.

When God has a plan for your life it doesn't have to make sense. Jesus told me in prayer that He was going to heal me but not until He took me down first. This was apparently necessary because He told me, *If I don't take you down first, people won't believe it when I bring you back up.*

Jesus said, *I want you to tell your testimony every day.* He said, *When I get through with you won't even have the smell of smoke. The only way people will know you have MS it is when you open your mouth.* My Testimony would be my life support and God promised that He would keep me well through the journey.

After that, my health deteriorated rapidly until I was almost blind, my speech had deteriorated, and my kidneys were failing. I was down like a baby. I couldn't do anything for myself, not even eat, or dress myself. I was using a walker to get around. Finally, my doctor prescribed a wheelchair. He offered no hope for me. But when I realized that this was how my life would end, I knew I wanted to live and that I would do anything to survive. At the time of diagnosis, I was 50 pounds overweight. I went from a size 16 to a 4 in just a few months. I just had to beat "Missy," which was the nickname I gave to this terrible disease, and I was willing to do anything to stay out of that wheelchair.

I prayed so hard. After that, God gave me a miracle. I met a couple Jeffrey & Krasandra Holmes who had the hope I so desperately needed. They said it would be the hardest thing I would ever do in my life, but that if I wanted to live, they could help me. They gave me an alternative treatment that consisted of no medications and a change in eating habits and lifestyle. This treatment involved eating a Vegan diet with no diary, meat, or white flour and sugar products.

It took a year of hard struggles and I wanted to quit many times, but the treatment worked! My vision started returning and my kidneys started working again. The joy I thought I had lost slowly started to return. Today I am living a life free from symptoms thanks to an excellent support group, lifestyle changes, and a strict regimen of exercise along with the Vegan diet that this couple shared with me.

When my doctor saw me just one year later, he didn't recognize me. He said that my recovery is nothing short of a miracle and he was shocked that I did it drug free. His prognosis predicted that I would be blind, would never walk again, and that I would be dead within one year. He couldn't believe the vision standing before him; thin, glowing and happy. And when I told him how I had gotten well, he didn't believe me.

Today, I walk a minimum of 8 miles per week and I have lots of energy. This is miraculous considering the fact that death was the next step for me after the wheelchair. I never felt better. I have moved on to a productive life. I have an exciting career and I enjoy volunteering at non-profits my church, and singing in the choir, but my main focus is sharing my story of healing without drugs or medical assistance with other people who are suffering from Multiple Sclerosis OR other diseases.

People are also sharing my story with others. These people contact me and I have the opportunity to talk with them to encourage and help them as well. I communicate directly with people afflicted with MS on the Internet, Facebook and in person who are interested in a holistic approach to their health and believing in the impossible.

The support I received during this time came from family, friends, and my wonderful husband, Jeff. The result was that people saw me overcome death and this was a faith builder for many people with the disease, and still is. When I stopped worrying about tomorrow and began to cling to my God in a process that showed me how to concentrate on one day at a time, I was able to live in the moment. This broke my healing process down in to manageable pieces, and after 3 years of pain and struggle, I emerged a whole person and got my life back.

Going through this experience has shown me a lot about myself. I have seen and experienced the awesome power of God. In the beginning I was very angry with God. But later on I realized that the person I was mad at was the only person who could heal me. What I thought came to kill me actually came to heal me. MS has made me stronger than ever before. I tell more people about Jesus than ever before and how good He has been to me. I never used to testify about Jesus before this diagnosis.

Through my healing process Jesus taught and showed me many things. He told me the only way He could heal me was if I learn how to forgive those who hurt me. I immediately began to forgive them. I even called people with whom I had a strained relationship and ask had I done anything wrong. God has taken me to levels I never could have imagined and has allowed me to do things I thought were impossible.

Before my dad passed away 4/29/09, he told to take this to another level. To date, I have been featured in September 2010 Career Magazine Edition of Movers & Shakers under 40. I captained my first MS Walk Team in April 2011 working on my third in dedication to my father, Andre Carter. Our team was named DIVAAS Divine Inspirational Virtuous Anointed Andreka. The MS Walk is the largest fundraiser the MS Society Sponsors. I also received the 2012 Multiple Sclerosis Leadership Award for Business Leaders making a difference which is the highest award from the MS Society. After receiving the MS Leadership Award for all of the recipients were featured in May 2012 Atlanta Business Chronicle.

My Job in life now is to be a blessing wherever this journey leads me. I always tell people during the darkest time in your life you have to find a song. Whatever Season I'm in, God always gives me a song for the sorrow. You never come out of your dark times without God giving you some new light to cherish. I have learned when you pray with a right spirit, your prayer will move the hands that control the world. I have learned to pray with a bold spirit and a faith-filled and forgiving heart. I never want to miss out on God's best because I am afraid to ask.

MS keeps a person from moving. But for me, MS was the catalyst that <u>got</u> me moving. Today, I am a Diabetic Medical Account Executive for Chronic Health Management for the prevention and management of diabetes. This was the perfect fit for me I'm able to share and educate the people I serve every day. The people I serve are the joys and loves of my life, and I have suffered some of the same things my patients are going through.

I have learned not to be pushed by my problems, but to be lead by God's promises and His purpose and plan. I always have remembered to pray God's highest favor on my Life just like my Mama Janice said. This helps me to enrich other's lives right along with mine. I learned to take the limits off of God and let him do what is best for me. I have learned the only thing that will limit God is me.

God told me before I saw my brain 2/20/09 my entire brain is now covered with legions that He was the same God that kept *Shadrach, Meshach, and Abednego from getting burned in the fiery furnace.* He said he kept Daniel in the lion's den from being eaten and kept the children of Israel from drowning in the Red Sea. He said he raised Lazarus from the grave. Then He said, *Andreka why don't you think I can keep you from MS? I'm God. I heal the way I want to heal. Compassion and passion is always born out of pain.*

THANK YOU

I want to first thank my Heavenly Father for dying for me, showing me my purpose, giving my life purpose and meaning, to be a blessing to others. I would like to dedicate this book to the memory of the people who help make me what I am today who are no longer here: My daddy Andre M. Carter, my grandparents, Bennie and Rosa Carter and Willie Mack and Marietta Turner and my great-grandmother, Kitty Ann Atwater. They showed me what serving others is all about. They taught and showed me how to love others in spite of their actions and how to use my gift of faith.

I want to thank my wonderful husband Jeff Eberhart for staying by my side through these difficult times and helping me through the rough times in my life. I want to thank my mother, Janice Carter for telling me and showing me my gifts of faith at a very early age in life. I also thank my parents for giving me a christian education which helped me to heal and grow spiritually.

Tarron (Tracey) &Tiffany Carter my siblings, I thank you for the love and keeping me grounded. I thank my "ride or die BFF's" for over 25 years of friendship. I thank Kristea and Quinton Cancel and Shavonne and Jeff Ladonis for making sure that I got to the hospital and encouraging me through my suicidal moments. To Jeff and Krasandra Holmes, I thank you for sharing the miracle of healing with me. I would like to thank also my very supportive friend, Dionne Carter and Cherisse & Cleo Atwaters, who always encourage and support me. I would like to take time out to give a special thanks to my family and friends for praying and loving me through this very difficult life journey. I want to give a special thanks to my cousin/sis. Kita (Joe) Wilson for the love and coming to the ER on September 5, 2003. You waited all night until I got answers. I want to thank my cousins/siblings came to make sure that I was alright: Charvette Shumaker,Meka Miller, Chandra Turner, Keisha Turner, Michael Paul Tinch & Darren Tinch. I want to thank also my church family, the Atlanta Maranatha SDA Church. I also would like to thank the World Church, the Seventh Day Adventist Church family for this health message and the world wide prayers on my behalf for my healing which has helped save my life. I also would like to give a special thanks to Chronic Health Management,

MS Society GA Chapter, Diabetes Association,Quest 35 Supportive Housing, Genesis Supportive Services and Southeastern Ambulance who have allowed me to use my God given gifts. Thanking the loves of my life, the people that I serve every day, my patients. I thank also my MS WALK TEAM DIVAAS for supporting me. I love each and every one of you from the bottom of my heart and appreciate the outpouring of love, encouragement and support.

Special thanks to God Almighty, who is the beginning and the end of my life. Thanks to my wife, who God has set before my life. Thanks to my sister and my brother in law who are the pastors of my life, and thanks to all the many friends as well as enemies, who strengthened my life.

Marc E. Willis

To Phyllis Willis, a song of love. You are the sunshine of my life. You bring me joy when there is strife. Sometimes I feel like I will cry, but you're there to dry my eyes. Sometimes when the sunshade is gloom, you call me to the bedroom, then I begin to smile, cause I know the day is about to be wild. Ah-Men! Hal-le-lu-jah!!

CLOSING

From the beginning until the end, God has this all under control; our growing up from one to one hundred years of age. From our broken legs and our misguided walks to our healing and learning to run, God has never forsaken us.

Out of all the testimonies you have read, all share one strong and powerful similarity, and that is that God loves us so much that He sent His only son to die for all our sins and whosoever believe on Him, shall gain everlasting life. Therefore, every sickness every worry and every tear that comes upon us, we have the power to change the outcome of any situation.

God requires that we exercise the fruits of the spirit and with that, power is immediately transferred to us. Learn to trust in the power of God and lean not into what you see, feel or hear, but believe in God's understanding and all that He gives.

Keep a fertile mind, always giving birth to a stronger inner desire to do better in life and that desire will be achieved. Band together and believe together, that through Christ, all things are possible.

Like every testimony in this book, it's only a testimony because God showed up and showed out in your situation. Faith, hope and belief is our saving grace.

IF AT FIRST YOU DIDN'T *BELIEVE* IN A HIGHER POWER,

DO YOU BELIEVE NOW?

Saved

By

Grace

A Book of Triumphs and Impossibilities

By
Marc Willis and
Andreka Eberhart